THE WOLFHOUND GUIDE
TO
The Shamrock

D0818466

THE WOLFHOUND GUIDE
TO
The Shamrock

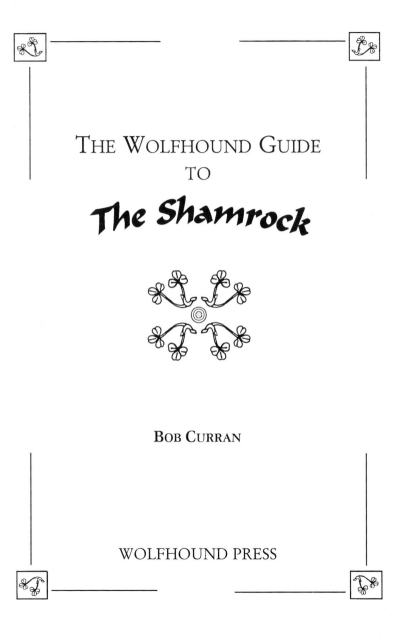

BOB CURRAN

WOLFHOUND PRESS

Published in 1999 by
Wolfhound Press Ltd
68 Mountjoy Square
Dublin 1, Ireland
Tel: (353-1) 874 0354
Fax: (353-1) 872 0207

British Library Cataloguing in Publication Data
A catalogue record for this book is available from the British Library.

ISBN 0-86327-726-8
10 9 8 7 6 5 4 3 2 1

Line Drawings: Ann Fallon
Cover Illustration: Nicola Emoe
Cover Design: Slick Fish Design, Dublin
Typesetting: Wolfhound Press
Printed by Edelvives, Spain

Contents

Introduction

No plant or growth is as closely associated with Ireland as the shamrock. In fact, it has become the very symbol of the country and of Irishness overseas. Its three-leafed form appears on Irish postcards, linen and tableware, and on mass-produced 'Irish' pottery and souvenirs — many of which are actually produced in other parts of the world. Symbolic references to the shamrock can also be found in Irish romantic poetry down through the ages and even in the heartfelt songs of misty-eyed Irish emigrants wherever they gather, be it London, New York or Sydney. In the emigrant tradition, it represents a permanent and tangible link with the country of their birth, its culture and history:

> *Farewell my old acquaintance, my friends both one and all,*
> *My lot is in America, to either rise or fall,*
> *From my cabin I'm evicted and likewise compelled to go,*
> *From that lovely land called Erin,*
> *Where the wild shamrocks grow.*
>
> Henry Glassie

The shamrock too, has a strong connection with Irish religion and with Ireland's patron saint, Patrick. Indeed, the saint is sometimes mistakenly credited with bringing the plant to the country from somewhere overseas on the soles of his sandals. At the very least, Patrick is traditionally believed to have both nurtured and named it:

> *There's a dear little plant that grows in our isle,*
> *'Twas St Patrick himself sure that set it,*
> *And the sun on his labours with pleasure did smile,*
> *And the dews from his eye oft did wet it.*
> *It thrives through the bog, through the brake, through the*
> *mireland,*
> *And he called it the dear little shamrock of Ireland.*
>
> Henry Glassie

The shamrock is therefore clearly associated with the feast day of the saint — Saint Patrick's Day (17 March) — and no self-respecting Irishman, according to tradition, should be abroad at that time without a sprig of the plant in his hat or lapel. It is also customary on that day to 'drown the shamrock' with a glass of spirits and for unbridled gaiety and celebration in honour of the plant, the saint and Ireland itself. The Reverend Fitzgerald and T.P. McGregor, in their *History, Topography and Antiquities of Limerick* state that in the city:

> *Patrick's-day commences with numerous acts of devotion at a*
> *well dedicated to the saint in the neighbourhood of the city and*
> *ends with copious libations to his memory.*

It is not surprising, given its close association with Ireland and its saint, that the shamrock should be strongly associated with Irish patriotism and, in some quarters, with rebellion against the English. Indeed, that great celebration of Irishness — the Saint Patrick's Day parade in New York, on which shamrocks are worn like cockades by anyone with Irish connections — is often boycotted by Northern Unionists who consider themselves to be British and who see the plant as an emblem of Irish Republicanism.

Just as it bears three leaves, the shamrock combines the three elements of Irish life — the social/cultural, the religious and the political. Perhaps more than any other plant, in any other country, its own tradition typifies that of Ireland itself — the complicated social mix coupled with the tortuous history. This is summed up in the words of the 'national lyricist of Ireland', Thomas Moore, in 1812:

Oh the shamrock, the green immortal shamrock!
Chosen leaf,
Of Bard and Chief,
Old Erin's native shamrock.

'Moore: 'Oh the Shamrock!'

With all this rich and deeply-felt heritage, it might be imagined that any cultural, social and political history of the shamrock might be extremely easy to research and quite easy to write. This, however, is far from the case, for the shamrock's history has been both a complicated and confusing one. There have been arguments concerning its spelling, its classification as a plant and the meaning of its symbolism — which has been used by both Unionists and Republicans alike — and it has actually been used on a number of occasions to denigrate and defame the Irish. In fact, although much poetry and many songs have been written in its praise, very little has actually been written concerning the origins of the shamrock tradition and its place in Irish history. The source material, therefore, remains remarkably sketchy. Indeed, there is really only one main authoritative source from which any scholar can draw. This is the work of an amateur naturalist who worked as a clerk at the Dublin Metropolitan Police Courts at the end of the last century. His name was Nathaniel Colgan and he is probably one of the very few people to have conducted a serious study regarding the identity of the shamrock and to have detailed at least part of its chronology and its place in the historical context of Ireland.

To classify the plant at the end of the last century, Colgan asked several persons living in different parts of Ireland to send him living, rooted specimens of the 'real shamrock' from their districts. All of these he carefully planted and labelled. When the plants matured and blossomed, Colgan noted that there was no doubt as to what they were. There were, in all, four different types of plants represented in his collection and he called in a number of other prominent Dublin horticulturists

Shamrock design on hand-stiched Carrickmacross Lace.
Lace-making in Carrickmacross dates back to 1820.
Courtesy Carrickmacross Lace, County Monaghan.

to confirm his findings. The majority of the opinion favoured that many of the plants were *Trifolium repens* (ordinary white clover) and *Trifolium minor* (lesser trefoil clover). There was also *Trifolium pratense* (purple clover) and *Medicago lupulina* (black medick). Colgan's classification of the shamrock is still accepted today.

Much of shamrock history, however, remains shrouded in mystery. Even the name itself does not give us any real clues as to its origins. In fact, the word 'shamrock' was not used at all until around the beginning of the fourteenth century. Early Irish manuscripts use the classification *Seamair* or *Seamrach*, signifying clover, to describe the plant and it is taken that the name of the plant comes from the ancient Irish *seamróg* or *seamair óg*, meaning 'young clover'. However, the earliest references to the shamrock usually come in the form of an adjective — *seamrach* — which is generally taken to mean 'clover-covered'. The manuscripts also usually combine the word with *scoth*, meaning a flower or tuft, to form the poetic description *scothsheamrach* (clover-flowered). It is in this poetic form that the word first appears in medieval Irish texts, although there are many variations as to its spelling and grammatical context.

In its earliest form, the word 'shamrock' is closely associated with poetry. Its first mention, as far as we can ascertain, appears in the *Metrical Dindsenchas* — a collection of miscellaneous poems which recount the legends, myths and lore surrounding certain place names from all over the country. This collection is thought to date from around the mid-to late-1300s, although some of the poems are undoubtedly of far greater antiquity and certainly predate medieval times by several centuries. One of these poems concerning Temair Luachra near Castleisland in County Kerry, contains the following description:

> . . . *nos fuilngtis a scothshemair.* . . .
> (its flowering clover beneath their feet)

In a second poem from the same source, reputedly commemorating a great and famous fair at Tailtin (Teltown, County Meath), we read:

> . . . *ba mag Scoth semrach.* . . .
> (it became a plain blossoming with flowering or tufted clover)

Shamrock, then, becomes a word of Irish origin which appears to have been used, even in medieval times, to describe clover, although whether it referred to clover in general or to a specific clover-type is not altogether clear.

Despite seeming to be inextricably linked with clover, even in the ancient mind, fierce disagreements as to its actual classification raged during the seventeenth and eighteenth centuries — although these had more to do with political propaganda than an actual determination of the plant.

While the medieval references to shamrock are widely scattered and show no real cohesion, there is still a strong suspicion that, even in these early times, the plant played some significant part in Irish social and cultural life. Why else should it have rapidly assumed such a central position in the Irish imagination? Why else would Saint Patrick have used that particular growth (if use it he did) to explain to the pagan Irish the fundamental Truth of the Trinity? And why was such teaching so readily accepted? Does the shamrock actually have a longer history than the infrequent glimpses from medieval verse would suggest? Whilst we may have no real answers to these questions we can, nevertheless, make a series of informed guesses regarding its tradition and it is to these that we now turn our attention.

Chapter One

The Pagan Tradition

No primary source material has come down to us from pagan Ireland, so it is difficult to estimate the importance of the shamrock (or even of clover) within the earliest societies in the country. The Celts themselves wrote nothing, and historians have therefore come to rely upon classical authors for their pictures of the Celtic world. However, apart from some coastal trading settlements, the Romans did not occupy Ireland to any great extent, so there was little chance to observe the customs and traditions of the people there. No references to the shamrock exist in the great Myth Cycles of Ireland or in any of the tales concerning major Irish heroes. Nor can any formal mention of it be found in the annals of the classical writers — although Pliny, in his *Natural History*, written in the first century AD, does remark that clover was widely regarded as a defence against snakes and that no serpent would even approach the growth.

Nevertheless, there must have been some tradition handed down from generation to generation concerning the plant. We can make this assumption from the later traditions which were often ascribed to both the shamrock and clover, both in Ireland and in other parts of the formerly Celtic world.

In Britain, clover held an ambivalent tradition. It was said by some to be a 'fairy growth', whilst others regarded it as an infallible protection against the fairies. The British folklorist Katharine Briggs states that clover (particularly the four-leafed kind):

> . . . is chiefly used to dissolve glamour (magically induced hallucination) in spells cast either by fairies or magicians. The fairy ointment which enabled mortals to see through the glamorous appearance of the fairies was said to be compounded from the (four-leaf) clover.

Ireland, too, shared a similar belief in the powers of both clover and shamrocks against fairy magic. It was believed, for example, in parts of the Glens of Antrim, that a mixture of clover and whiskey massaged into the eyes would lift the 'fairy blindness' caused by malignant sprites. Meanwhile, on Rathlin Island it used to be said that pounded shamrock rubbed across the eyes would allow sight of a particular fairy island which was supposed to lie between Rathlin and the mainland at Ballycastle.

The use of the shamrock as a protection against the baneful forces of spirits and ancient gods appears in certain Irish healing stories. An oral tradition, which may come from a more ancient written source, still exists in the west of Ireland concerning the great warrior-healer of County Mayo, Foranan

O'Fergus. Although the stories are set in the Penal Times in Ireland and are strongly Christian in tone, they still contain many of the elements of the early mythical hero-tales and doubtless take their traditions from more pagan times. Indeed, their underlying function may well have been to pass down herbal medical lore from one generation to the next. One tale in particular mentions the use of the shamrock as an apotropaic against dark and ancient forces.

According to the legend, Foranan O'Fergus lived in Western Mayo about the beginning of the seventeenth century. His forebears had been trained in the ways of leechcraft and herbs by the O'Malleys of Mayo, who at one time had been the greatest physicians in all of Ireland, and this knowledge had been handed down to Foranan. Not only this, but he had married 'a dark woman of the Sidhe' (fairies) and had received from her 'the ancient learning of her people', particularly that which related to illness and exorcism. To balance things between the 'strange lore of the Sidhe' and the teachings of the Church, he carried under his clothing a holy scapular containing a fragment of bone from a saint. With the twin powers of paganism and Christianity behind him, Foranan became one of the most famed healers, not only in Ireland but in parts of England and Wales as well. The following extract is adapted from a Tipperary tradition. Foranan is called to the village of Cloonlara near the rugged Mayo coast to attend to a man who is believed to be dying.

The village was nothing more than a few cabins, hovels and sod-houses, tucked into the side of a tiny glen amongst the hills. It was a dark, bleak place where the black smoke of the hearths clouded the still air overhead and the stink of poverty attacked the traveller's nostrils. The houses were rude and dirty and many were in a state of pitiful disrepair. Richard O'Toole's house lay at the far end of the village street and was one of the smallest and roughest-looking dwellings there. As he went into the place, several old men crowded in after him to pay their respects to the great hero and healer.

Richard O'Toole lay in one dark corner of the dwelling on a pile of old coats and beside a small heap of dying coals. Because of his magical powers, Foranan could see a fever wrapped around him like a great coiled serpent in the half-light, drawing ever more tightly about his body. As he entered, it rose up slightly and although much of its body still seemed indistinct, its baleful eyes glinted fiercely, like deadly jewels. Foranan's dog, Flann, sensing the fever-serpent with the instinct of a hound, stayed by the door of the house and refused to come any further.

'Tell me', Foranan said to the old men. 'How did he come to be like this?'

'Musha, Healer', said one, 'it was his own fault altogether for he's a headstrong and contrary man. Over a fortnight ago and against all advice, he went to an old cave in the dark glen of Lugatharee down on the coast, for he thought that it might contain treasure left over from the Viking times. The cave is widely known as the dwelling place of an invisible spirit from years gone by, which takes revenge on all those who trespass on its ground. Even though he explored the greater part of the

cave, he found no treasure — only the jawbone of a donkey — but when he came out of the place, he was white and trembling as if he'd taken an awful chill. A couple of days afterwards, he took a fever that laid him low and he's not likely to lift his head again unless there's something that you can do for him. It's the curse of the cave spirit that he lies under surely'.

Foranan looked down at the sick man with the magical eye of druid knowledge, and the fever-serpent, well aware of his presence, flexed its body, silver scales rippling in the weak firelight, and bared long fangs at him. Unafraid, the healer thought for a moment.

'Bring me a handful of pin-meal, mixed with clover or mountain heather and uisce beatha *(whiskey) and a supeen of milk with pounded shamrock mixed into it and then we'll know if we can lift this affliction or not', he said to the old man who had spoken.*

The other hurried away to do his bidding whilst Foranan sat by the sick man's bed. 'There's nothing like the clover and the holy shamrock to drive out the evil spirits that afflict men', he remarked, half to himself and half to those who remained. And, all the while, the serpent-thing weaved and watched him with its glistening, jewel-like eyes and hissing softly to itself — a sound which only Foranan himself could hear. In the doorway behind him, Flann waited patiently, his hackles raised, refusing to come any further into the room.

Soon the men returned, bearing the remedies that Foranan had asked for. Taking from round his neck the holy relic, given him by Fr Lyons, the healer began to pass it back and forth over the dying man's brow to hold the fever at bay.

'Now', he said, 'give him the milk and the mashed sham-rock. Force it between his lips if you have to'. And they fed him some of the milky mixture on the end of a horn spoon. He took it grudgingly and, from time to time, they had to force it down. Seeing what was going on, the serpent tightened its coils even more tightly around the man, making him cry out with the pain. Foranan took the meal-mixture and the spoon and began to feed the man himself whilst the creature weaved and hissed above them and threatened to dart at him, its maw wide open. Again the scales rippled, the overall form of the thing seemed to grow hazy and less certain. The grip on the dying man seemed to loosen a little but the spirit-creature made no move to quit the body. Foranan knew then that Richard O'Toole was far too weak to drive out the fever and that it would probably kill him.

'It must be a very powerful spirit indeed', he murmured to himself, 'for both clover and the shamrock are always a sover-eign remedy against fevers and spirit-things of this kind'. The serpent rose up over the body and filled the narrow house with its hissing, although all those that were gathered close by heard nothing. Only Flann, sensing that something was wrong, bared his teeth and growled deep in his throat.

'Well now', said Foranan, sliding the holy relic beneath his clothes once more, 'the charm of the clover and the sham-rock hasn't broken the fever on him at all. Send for your parish priest, Fr Lorcan O'Cassidy, to hear his Confession and to prepare him for Eternity, for he will live only about another week. His body is far too frail and the fever has got too strong a hold on him. Had you sent for me sooner, I would have driven it away with my holy artefacts and clover-charm

but now that he's well in its grip, there's little that I can do.
Go and bring Fr Lorcan here now'.

And so saying, he gathered his cloak around him and set
off for home across the barren uplands. The old men accompa-
nied him to the edge of the village and, after kissing his hand
and the hem of his coat as a mark of their great respect, they
watched him as he strode off across the hills. Soon he had dis-
appeared from their view, his hound at his heels.

Adapted by the author from traditional
sources in his own collection: Tipperary

The story is worth recounting because it contains references to the traditional use of clover and shamrock in 'charms'
to drive away fevers caused by malicious and harmful spirits.

A similar tale concerns a famous County Cork piper,
Garrett Barry. Like Foranan O'Fergus he also used the shamrock to drive away dark forces. This tale is believed to have
come down, almost unaltered, from the late nineteenth century:

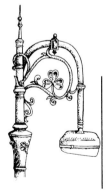

There was no other musician who could
play so sure a note or so sweet a melody as
Garrett Barry but it was said that all his
music, beautiful as it was, was stolen from
the fairies. Garrett wandered about
Ireland with his pipes across his back, play-
ing at wakes, fairs and céilís as travelling
pipers did in those days, and in the course
of his travels he would come to some old
fairy fort or rath or some ruined castle

which was said to be inhabited by the fairy-kind. He would wait there until nightfall, until the fairies would come out and play their tunes; then he would copy them, note for note. This made him extremely famous, for the tunes that he copied were the old, old tunes of Ireland that the people had all but forgotten and his playing was so fine and so exquisite that it brought many a tear to an ancient eye. Oh, but it was a dangerous occupation all right, for the fairies do not take very kindly to mortal musicians who steal their tunes and are always looking out to do them harm. But Garrett Barry, he didn't seem to care and showed no fear at all. He was a very religious man and never missed daily Mass (sometimes even going twice a day) and it stood to him, for the fairies seemed to have no power over him.

One time, he was playing at a céilí away in the County Sligo and he overheard a number of old men talking about a well in a remote part of the country. Although there are the ruins of an old church there, the well itself was a pagan one. Anyway, Garrett Barry heard that the country people would go nowhere near this well after dark for it was surrounded by low-hanging and gloomy trees and the voice of an invisible spirit could be heard singing there in the evening. It sang an ancient song and the rendition was said to be very beautiful. But it was an old god left over from pagan times and should not be approached. Garrett made up his mind to go down to the well and hear the song for himself. If it was as beautiful and melodic as the old men said, he would copy it down for himself. Because it was a haunted place, he decided to put a crucifix about his neck as a protection against whatever powers that might be lurking in the well-water.

So he approached the ruins of the old church, just as darkness was beginning to fall. The wind sighed among the nearby trees like an old man badly crippled with pains and the ruins looked very dark and menacing indeed. A faint mist hovered over the surface of the water, writhing and moving like something alive. Garrett sat down on a large stone near the well and set up his pipes. After a time, the wind dropped and he could hear a voice singing softly close to the water's edge. The tune was indeed very beautiful but he couldn't tell if it was a man or a woman who sang. Still, he picked up his pipes and began to follow the notes very closely.

But now the voice seemed to change slightly and an angry tone appeared to come into it. Garrett touched the crucifix about his neck for comfort but all the same he was beginning to feel a little uneasy. Without warning, the mist which had been gathering on the surface of the well formed into a long tentacle which shot out of the gloom and grabbed the piper around the middle, squeezing him with a powerful force. It had soon wrapped itself around him like a snake and seemed to be bent on killing him with its grip. At the same time, Garrett Barry's skin burned as if it had been flayed by a thousand knives and he knew that this was the spirit trying to show its displeasure at his stealing its tune. He grabbed the crucifix and muttered some sort of prayer but the grip around him tightened. The spirit which attacked him was far older than Christianity, you see, and so the holy protection had little effect on it. Garrett struggled and thought that his last day had indeed come. Then, in the half-light, he saw a small shamrock-covered hill close by and he reached out his hand to grasp a bunch of the holy plant. No sooner had his fingers touched the *growth than the mist let go of him and he fell forward to the ground. The voice in the well ceased to sing and Garrett stumbled up into the precincts of the old church and well away from the water's edge. He'd had a lucky escape and ever after, when he went round the forts, raths and ruined castles where the fairies dwelt to take down their tunes, he always wore a spring of shamrock or clover in his hatband as a protection against ancient evil. The voice in the well was never heard to sing again, although the well itself is still a very eerie place and few people will go near it, even yet.*

Adapted from traditional sources in the
author's own collection: County Sligo

In both these stories 'the clover (or shamrock) charm' has been employed to drive away ancient and primal forces, which hints at some long tradition originating in pagan times. It is also interesting to note that both the fever and the spirit-tentacle are described as being snake or serpent-like, recalling Pliny's assertion that clover can drive away snakes and act as a remedy for serpent bites.

As the Celts gradually became a primarily agricultural people, their knowledge and lore concerning herbs and plants increased. Just as modern-day medicine draws heavily upon the extracts of growing things as a basis for its drugs and preparations, early folk medical practitioners also sought their cures in the natural world. This practice continued in certain rural areas right up until the beginning of the present century because official medical help was often expensive or difficult to come by.

Folk practitioners with their bags of herbs and plants continued to thrive in country areas until within living memory.

Great 'herbals', detailing the uses of plants, were passed down and were sometimes consulted even by medical doctors across succeeding years. A massive compendium simply entitled *Elixirs*, reputedly written in 1552 by the sage Nostradamus, detailed both the medical and cosmetic uses of the extracts of over one thousand separate plants, and was allegedly much sought after by physicians in England and France. Many of the 'wonder drugs', antibiotics and tranquillisers used today have origins not all that far removed from the great natural herbals of the past.

Why did the plants work their wonderful cures? Today we would look for some scientific reason but to the Celtic mind, the answer was simple — they were directly connected to the gods or to the spirit world. Illness caused by the intervention of evil spirits could be cured by supplication to the gods and by the application of certain plants which they had provided for human use. Ivy leaves were said to cure corns and boils; the humble dock would cure bites and stings (particularly those of nettles); mistletoe would cure sterility (as well as being used by witches to create storms); foxgloves would cure epilepsy and palpitations of the heart.

A number of classical writers mention the healing ceremonies of the druids (the ancient Celtic holy men), which involved elaborate ritual and often animal sacrifice to the gods.

Caesar mentions that extracts from oak leaves, ivy and mistletoe were also closely associated with these types of ceremonies and were collected amid great ceremony at certain times of the year. Christianity continued the practice of identifying certain plants with holy ceremony — in the above story, for example, Foranan holds a sacred scapular whilst administering the 'clover charm' to the dying man.

Traditionally, the shamrock is closely associated with Christian principles (notably the Trinity) but it is possible that there were older associations with more pagan deities, primarily for healing purposes. In ancient Ireland there was indeed a much older Trinity than that which was brought by the Christian missionaries. There is no doubt that numbers played an important role in the ancient Celtic world and the most sacred or magical number was 'three'. The structure of Celtic society was classified in three ways — priests, warriors, agriculturists — whilst in Ireland and Wales, traditional teaching was carried out using 'concept clusters', each containing three truths. Irish legend abounds with the mystical number: there were three sons of Uisnech (although only Naoise, the lover of Deirdre, has any real identity); three Children of Lir; three sons of Tureen (all of these stories combining to make the Three Great Sorrows of Irish Storytelling); Cú Chulainn had his hair tied in triple braids and is recorded as killing his enemies in groups of three. In vernacular Irish folklore, the number occurs time and time again — three wishes, three sisters, three tasks.

Most importantly, there was the Celtic Triple-Goddess which appears to have been the central motif in many of the Irish mythological tales and in the beliefs of ancient Ireland. She was worshipped across the Celtic world and her shrines appear as far apart as Hungary and Britain. In Ireland, she was worshipped as the three-fold goddess of fertility, war and slaughter (in the form of Macha, the Badb and the Morrigu). Some historians have argued that as a fertility goddess she was known as Brigid, the goddess of Imbolc (a spring festival performed around 2 February), worshipped chiefly in Leinster, and was the pagan prototype for the saint of the same name. Legend states that Saint Brigid also had two sisters, both of whom were druidesses. In her most fundamental state the Triple-Goddess represented the three stages of human existence — birth, life and death. Her three Irish counterparts — Macha, Badb and Morrigain (Morrigu) were all female in gender and were all interchangeable, sometimes appearing as a beautiful young woman, sometimes as a stately matron and sometimes as a screaming old hag. The three goddesses in one presided over ancient battlefields, ensuring victory to those who worshipped them, by 'intoxicating' them with battle frenzy and sometimes even healing their wounds at the end of the conflict.

Numerous Celtic spirits and deities possessed three manifestations and their images have been found all over the Celtic world. Amongst those were the Genii Cucullati ('Hooded Spirits'), fertility spirits mainly found in Gaul (France), and

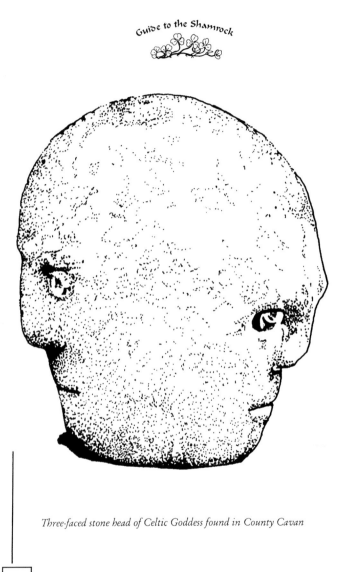

Three-faced stone head of Celtic Goddess found in County Cavan

usually depicted wearing long hooded capes. Hidden under these hoods were three faces, each representing a different aspect of the spirit. These became strongly associated with the hooded missionary monks who came to Ireland from Gaul. Such mysterious spirits were usually associated with renewal and healing, and were still being worshipped during the early Christian period.

Given the close association between spirits and plants it is not difficult to imagine that the three-leafed clover or shamrock was suggestive of the Triple-Goddess or of triple-spirits, and that this supernatural attachment formed the basis of the 'clover charm'. It probably stretched into the dim pagan past, long before the coming to Ireland of Saint Patrick. The three leaves represented the three separate goddesses, unified into a single entity (and plant) by the stem. It was this originally pagan motif that Patrick himself is alleged to have used to great effect when explaining the concept of the Christian Trinity.

One of the foremost functions of the Triple-Goddess was that of healing, particularly the healing of those who had fallen during a battle. Using these herbs, practitioners of the healing arts may have deliberately called upon the Macha aspect of the Triple-Goddess to staunch excessive bleeding or relieve the effects of sword blows. Indeed, the first 'hospital' was traditionally held to have been situated at Ard-Macha (Macha's height) which was later to become the Irish ecclesiastical capital of

Armagh. A legend persists that, even after the coming of Christianity, an Ogham library comprising many of the great cures and tracing the relationship between plants and spirits, written on scrolls of tree bark, was maintained within the Holy See. Whatever the truth of this, it is well known that Irish healers and herbalists were much sought after for their skills with potions and powders right across the Western world until the Middle Ages. This library was subsequently destroyed during the reign in Armagh and Meath of the Viking tyrant Turgesius in the ninth century.

Might not the shamrock have been considered to be a curative plant, strongly associated with the Macha aspect of the Triple-Goddess? Certainly the story of Foranan O'Fergus would suggest at least some form of tradition regarding the growth, stretching far back beyond Christian times. It might not have been purely by chance that the early Christian missionaries used the plant as a means of explaining the Godhead to a pagan congregation. While this is pure speculation, it could mean that there is a much longer history to the shamrock than records would suggest. The legendary tradition of the shamrock in Ireland may, in fact, predate the arrival of Christianity in the fifth century.

Chapter Two

The Christian Tradition

According to tradition, Christianity was brought to Ireland by Saint Patrick who overcame the pagan druids of the Irish High King at Tara and then used the shamrock to explain the Mystery of the Trinity to the Irish. So ingrained in the Irish mind has this tradition become that it has almost assumed the status of historical fact.

In fact, the shamrock is so closely associated with the saint that it is usually worn as a badge of Irishness upon his festival day (17 March). And yet, there is no mention of the plant in any of the early Irish Christian writings or in the various 'Lives' of Patrick. There is also no suggestion that he actually used the shamrock to teach the Mystery as the legends state. Indeed, there is nothing at all to connect the shamrock and Saint Patrick. And even the personage of the saint himself is open to question.

So, how did the shamrock acquire its strongly Christian connections and how did it come to be identified with this particular saint? There is no doubt that the plant does have Christian connotations in Ireland, but they may be much deeper and more complicated than we might expect. In order

to speculate upon what they might be, we must first look at the person and message of Patrick himself.

> *I Patrick . . . had as my father Calpornius, son of the late Potitus, a priest who belonged to the town of Bannaviem Taberniae; he had a small estate nearby. . . .*
>
> A.B.E. Hood

Thus Patrick begins an account of his life and this seems straightforward enough. He was born at Bannaviem Taberniae into a wealthy Christian family, kidnapped by Irish pirates and sold into slavery in Ireland. He later escaped and fled to Gaul but, following a vision, returned again as a missionary to convert the heathen inhabitants of the country. It is an exciting and logical account of a great preacher and Founding Father. And yet, few other saints have evoked such controversy as Patrick, for despite his Life, there is much confusion as to who he was and where he came from.

Where, for example, was Bannaviem Taberniae where Patrick's father had his estates? Some have claimed it as being in ancient Britain (making Patrick British), many more have claimed that it was near present-day Dumbarton (making Patrick Scottish) and, much more recently, there have been claims that it was in the West Country (perhaps making Patrick a Cornishman).

Where was Patrick taken to be a slave? The traditional story states that he was taken to North Antrim to herd swine on the slopes of Slemish Mountain but other claimants for that honour include such counties as Sligo and Waterford. When did he return to Ireland as a missionary? Some sources state the early fifth century, others say that it was not until slightly later. Patrick himself gives no dates. The site of his landing in the country is also open to question. In the north of Ireland, he is believed to have landed at Strangford Lough, but he is also said to have arrived in Wexford. Did he come alone? Some traditions say yes, others mention at least two helpers. How did he travel all over Ireland in one lifetime to found churches and anoint new bishops as the legends claim (in the fifth century, Ireland was thickly forested, boggy and mountainous, and travel was extremely difficult)? Did he use the shamrock to reveal Immortal Truths? Some traditions say that he did, others make no mention of it. Others still, say that it is little more than a legend added several centuries after Patrick's death.

The whole story is an extremely confusing one, which makes the shamrock's connections with Christianity rather tenuous and problematical. However, given its strong associations with Saint Patrick's Day, there must be some Christian context within which the plant can be set. To discover its fundamental significance, we must first examine the entire 'Patrick legend'. Here, as an Irishman, I must risk being branded as something of a heretic because I am about to suggest that Saint Patrick (as we understand him) might not have existed at all — or rather, he may not have existed in the way in which we think that he did. Rather than being one man, the saint might have been a combination of three men.

We can say with some degree of confidence that Patrick was not the first Christian missionary to be active in Ireland. Missionaries had been arriving in the country from Christian settlements in Romanised Britain, from Wales and from Scotland, for many years before he allegedly set foot on Irish soil. *The Book of Ballymote*, compiled around 1390 AD, mentions a certain Caranoc (Abbot of Candida Casa) as the first recorded Christian in Ireland. According to the ancient historian Prosper of Aquitaine, around 430 AD, a British Celt named Congar (or Docco), who was working as a missionary in Ireland, wrote to Pope Celestine I (422–432 AD), stating that the Irish were now suitable for a formalised mission and the appointment of a bishop. (Congar is also historically credited with compiling the first Irish Christian liturgy, an act often traditionally attributed to Saint Patrick.) There was a certain degree of urgency in his request because the Christian Church was in the grip of a serious heresy, which some missionaries were carrying with them into the far-flung corners of the Celtic world.

The heresy had its roots in the teachings of Pelagius who was undoubtedly the most influential British Christian of the time. He was born around 354 AD and, although the location of his birth is unknown, it is thought that he might have been born in Ireland. Saint Jerome (who was one of his foremost detractors) derides him as 'being stuffed with Irish porridge'. Pelagius went to Rome in 380 AD and was dismayed at the laxity of both religion and morals which he found amongst the Christians there. This laxity he blamed squarely on the doctrines expounded in the writings of the greatly respected early Church father, Augustine of Hippo (doctrines that haav since become formal Church dogma), which maintained that everything had been preordained by God. If the doctrine of pre-ordination was correct, the Church argued, why should any man strive towards salvation? Pelagius began to teach that salvation, whilst certainly a gift from God, was the responsibility of individual men and women who should seek to achieve it for themselves. In fact, he argued, Augustine had placed in peril the entire moral law of the Church — if people accepted the theory of predestination, then there was nothing to restrain them from sin. People must make their own way to God, irrespective of Church teaching. This teaching may have been based in the highly developed pagan Celtic notions of individual responsibility towards spirits, and was enthusiastically accepted in Celtic lands where some of the missionaries were working.

Seeing its dogma and authority being openly challenged in such a fashion, the Church pronounced Pelagius a heretic. Augustine's own followers condemned his theories as an attempt to re-establish druidism — the pre-Christian religion of the Celts. There may have been an element of truth in this, for the druid law had been a very moral one and the Pelagian doctrine was being widely taught in Ireland (where druid influence had lingered) and was being propounded enthusiastically. It was also widely believed in Rome that the early missionaries were further allowing the Irish to retain their pagan festivals and were, themselves, adopting druid laws and practices to assist in converting non-Christians.

Faced with the possible spread of the heresy and the retention of pagan ways, it was imperative that a Roman bishop was established to enforce the authority, orthodoxy and doctrine of the Church in Ireland — the first country outside the influence of the old Roman Empire to be Christianised. Celestine referred the matter to the great missionary centre at Auxerre with instructions that a bishop be sent to Ireland right away. Auxerre, under the rule of its abbot, Saint Germanus, was undoubtedly an early 'nursery' to the missions, from which brethren went out all across the Celtic world. Germanus chose a particularly able ambassador — a Gaulish Celt named Palladius who had been acting as a deacon at the monastery for some years. Following Germanus's instructions, Palladius set out for Ireland straight away. He was 'the first bishop to the Irish believing in Christ' and bore the title 'Patricius' (Father).

It is here that history becomes rather hazy. Scholars disagree strongly as to whether or not Palladius actually reached

Ireland. Professor Thomas O'Rahilly, on the one hand, argues that Palladius never arrived in Ireland at all but succumbed to a plague which was raging in Britain at the time, dying there about 431 AD. On the other hand, Professor James Carney argues that Palladius did, in fact, reach Ireland and that he preached there for several years, aided by three other missionaries from Rome — Secondinius, Auxillius and Isernius. Professor Carney further argues that it was Secondinius who founded the great religious centre at Armagh (previously an important pagan site) in 444 AD, which was later to become the seat of the Irish Primacy, and that it was he (Secondinius) who was perhaps its first bishop. Certainly we can argue that Isernius was already in Ireland long before Palladius's arrival, as he had been imprisoned by Ende Censelah, a petty king of Leinster, and was released only upon 'the arrival of the Patricius' and the conversion to Christianity of one of the king's grandsons.

If Palladius did preach in Ireland, the period of his ministry did not last long. Ireland was gripped by plague and it is possible that he died in its throes in the early 440s, with his mission only partly completed.

A replacement had to be found and that task was referred once more to Saint Germanus at Auxerre. Palladius' successor was a British Celt named Sucat, reputedly born at Alcluyd (Dumbarton) into a Christian community there. He also bore the title 'Patricius'. This missionary would appear to have been the Patrick of the 'Tripartite Life' and the 'Confessio'. His father was a Christian deacon who used the Latinised name Calpurnicus and, early in life, he seems to have been taken prisoner by Irish raiders who carried him back with them to their own country. There he was forced to herd either sheep or swine in 'a lonely place' before eventually escaping, fleeing to Gaul (France) where he joined the important Christian settlement at Lerins, and becoming a deacon in the church. From Lerins, he travelled to Auxerre to study under Germanus, who eventually chose him to lead a new mission to Ireland. The date of his mission is hotly disputed — Carney suggests that it took place in 456 AD, whilst O'Rahilly argues that it occurred in 461 AD. He is reported to have landed in Strangford Lough in the north of Ireland, having come by way of his home in the kingdom of Strathclyde, with at least one follower, Seginis.

Sucat was by far the most effective of all the missionaries sent, and appears to have been an extremely able bishop. He was relatively familiar with Ireland, he spoke the language, he knew the ways of the people and he knew the geographical locations of a network of missions which had already been set up within the country by Palladius and his predecessors. Whether or not he travelled all over Ireland as is often claimed is unknown but it is highly unlikely that he did. Nevertheless, his followers — those whom he had consecrated as bishops — went about in his name, taking for themselves the title

*Ballyscunnion residents enjoying a Saint Patrick's Day pint
while sporting the shamrock.*
Courtesy Bronte Matthews and Donnatilla Elmes

'Patricius', bringing the Christian message to the Irish. Soon Irish monks were travelling back into Europe and further afield as missionaries themselves.

The third contender for the name of Patrick is a much more shadowy figure. He is also known to have predated Sucat (and perhaps Palladius), although he was not a bishop. He is Ibar and was certainly running a mission station in County Louth in 460 AD. He may have been Welsh but more likely was a Briton, the pupil of an even earlier missionary called Mocteus, a British Celt who must have come to Ireland directly from Rome, together with three Munstermen (who had been consecrated as Roman bishops), perhaps around 440 AD. Like both Palladius and Sucat, he seems to have been a very capable missionary leader and references to him are to be found in *The Book of Ballymote* and *The Book of Leinster*. However, relatively little is known about him, except that he was one of the earliest missionaries in the country and that he too styled himself 'Patricius' in Roman fashion. In fact, the title was widely used by many of the early Church fathers in Ireland. Saint Enda, Abbot of Killeany (530 AD) is reported to have gone to Rome with two companions, Ailbe and Puteus, where all three were baptised by Pope John II as 'Patrici of the Irish'. Similarly, Saint Fintan of Clonard may have used the title as did Erlatheus, Bishop of Armagh, at the end of the fifth century.

Thus, 'Patrick' may not initially have been a proper name at all, but rather a Roman title, which gradually became formalised into a name. Adopted as a nomenclature by the early bishops, over the years they took it as their own personal name. The title was very strongly identified with the Christian religion in Ireland and in its first inception may have referred to the three founders of the Christian Church in the country.

So how does all this sit with our notion of the shamrock? Just as the three leaves of the plant, springing from the one stem, may have been suggestive of the Triple-Goddess, so they may also have represented the three early Fathers of the Church (the original Patrici) — Ibar, the missionary, and Palladius and Sucat, the first bishops. All men sprang from the one source — the Christian faith as exemplified by the Roman Church, which united them as surely as the stem of the shamrock. And what of the legend in which Patrick (or one of the Patrici) explained the Mystery of the Trinity using the plant? If the legend is true, it may have been no great effort for the pagan Irish to accept the Triple-Deity which the Patricii brought with them. After all, they had already been worshipping a triple female deity of which the shamrock may have been the embodiment. It was no mere accident that the Christian missionaries chose the shamrock as their example.

Thus the shamrock embodied in its three leaves and one stem the history, tradition and theology of the incoming Christian faith. The three founding missionaries, united by one religion, soon coalesced into a more generalised 'Saint Patrick' with whom the growth was associated. He was allocated a specific feast day, but this in itself presented problems. Saint Patrick's Day fell within the period of Lent when his followers were expected to observe a strict abstinence. The feast day was supposed to be spent in pious reflection on the saint's life and works in Ireland, although in the late twelfth century, the Lenten restrictions on the eating of meat were slightly relaxed. Writing in 1186, the Cistercian scribe Jocelin of Furness makes reference to the sombre festival of Saint Patrick, on which day nothing was to be eaten but 'Saint Patrick's Fishes' (cold meat which was soaked in water and 'dressed to eat'). It was only much later that strong drink (now a feature of the festivities) could be taken and the festival became a raucous and joyous occasion. A traveller in Ireland, Thomas Dinely in his *Journal*, which seems to have been written around 1681, notes:

The 17th day of March yeerly is St. Patrick's, an immoveable feast when the Irish of all stations and condicions wore crosses in their hats, some of pins, some of green ribbon, and the vulgar superstitiously wear shamrogues, 3-leafed grasse, which they likewise eat (they say) to cause a sweet breath. The common people and servants also demand their St. Patrick's groat of their masters, which they goe expressly to towne, though half a dozen miles off, to spend, where sometimes it amounts to a piece of 8 or cobb a piece, and very few of the zealous are to be found sober at night.

Dinely and a number of other travellers through Ireland all draw attention to the drunken festivities of the former holy day but all mention that, as a token of sanctity, the Saint Patrick's Day Cross was worn by everyone, regardless of rank or station. Shamrocks, all writers agree, were worn only by the vulgar and superstitious.

The Saint Patrick's Day Cross was worn on the lapel, the shoulder or on the band of a hat in the saint's honour. It was usually handmade and was prepared about a week or so before the festival.

> *The 'St. Patrick's Cross' for boys consists of a small sheet of white paper, about three inches square, on which is inscribed a circle which is divided by elliptical lines or radii and the spaces thus formed are filled in with different hues, thus forming a circle of many coloured compartments.*
>
> *The little girl's 'St. Patrick's Day Cross' — which is made by an elder sister, or if sufficiently skilled, by herself — is formed by two pieces of card-board or strong, thick paper, about three inches long which are placed across at right angles, forming a cross humette. These are wrapped or covered with silk or ribbon of different colours, and a bunch or rosette of green silk in the centre which completes the tasteful little girl's 'St. Patrick's Cross' which is pinned to the bosom or shoulder.*
>
> Journal of the Cork Historical and
> Archaeological Society: 1895

Crosses made of twig (similar in style to the Saint Brigid's Cross) were also hung from the doorways and interior thatches of rural cottages on the feast day of the saint and this custom was extremely widespread. The *Journal of the Cork Historical and Archaeological Society* further reports:

> *I have counted over thirty such twig crosses in the houses of some of my acquaintances where old customs still prevail.*

Gradually, however, sprigs of shamrock began to replace the crosses as symbols of the saint, perhaps because of the strong Christian connections that the plant was already adopting, coupled with a long pagan tradition stretching back across time. Or it might be that the crosses themselves were becoming ever more elaborate and were too time-consuming to make. For whatever reason, by the early eighteenth century, sprigs and bunches of shamrock had almost completely replaced

the Saint Patrick's Day Cross as a symbol on the lapels and bosoms of the Irish people. It is also suggested by some writers that the shamrock was being processed, as a Christian symbol, through the towns and villages of Ireland on the saint's day and on other religious festivals.

Although the plant was now closely associated with Patrick, he was not the only saint to feature in shamrock legends. Around 1411, the Irish scribe Murchadh Ó Cuindlis, penned a volume entitled *An Leabhar Breac* (The Speckled Book). This had been commissioned by the influential MacAodhagan (MacEgan) family of County Galway and was written under their patronage. The book is a collection of ancient tales (probably drawn from vernacular sources) with a strong religious theme running through them. In one of the shorter stories, which refers to the saints Scuthin and Barra, Murchadh Ó Cuindlis makes specific references to the shamrock:

On one occasion he [Saint Scuthin] met Barra of Cork when he was walking on the sea and Barra was in a boat.
'Why do you walk on the sea?' asked Barra.
'It is not the sea', answered Scuthin, 'but a vast plain, flowery and shamrock-bearing (scothemrach)'. And bending down he picked a purple flower and threw it to Barra in the boat, at the same time asking 'Why then does a ship swim on the plain?' Then Barra put his hand over the side of the boat and hooked a salmon which he threw to Scuthin'.

Colgan: 'The Shamrock in Literature'

The above may be no more than a 'good word' (a joke, riddle or pleasant story), commonly told amongst churchmen, but it serves to illustrate that the shamrock was now featuring in some of the religious stories of the day, thus reinforcing its links with formalised Christianity.

Having perhaps started out as a pagan plant, emphasising a Triple-Goddess of the early Celts, the shamrock was now acquiring a strong Christian tradition. It would later reflect the change in both the religious and political mood of Ireland. The shamrock was entering a new era.

Chapter Three

A Period of Confusion

As a symbol, the shamrock was now poised to enter the political arena. As early at the beginning of the seventeenth century, we find mention of it in connection with those who left Ireland during the Flight of the Earls.

In 1607, the last of the ancient Gaelic aristocracy and tradition fell, following the failure of the rebellion of Hugh O'Neill, Earl of Tyrone, a man claimed by some to have been 'the last true king of Ireland'. For a number of years, O'Neill had waged war against English objectives in Ireland and the excesses of the Ulster Plantation in the North, and he had nearly succeeded in driving at least some of the planters out of the country. Nearly — but not quite — defeated by the new Viceroy of Ireland, Lord Mountjoy, more or less abandoned by his Spanish allies, and with his popularity in the Irish countryside gradually ebbing away, he was forced to make peace with his former enemies. In 1603, he signed a peace treaty with the Earl of Essex and, although partly restored to his former lands, thereafter was subject to English surveillance and harassment. The situation rapidly became intolerable — he could not, he declared, even drink a cup of sack (wine) without it being reported in London. Soon he could stand it no longer. In September 1607, with many of his supporters and retinue, Hugh O'Neill boarded a French ship in Lough Swilly, bound for the Continent, leaving Ireland behind forever. The event was known as the Flight of the Earls (the Earl of Tyrconnell also departed on the same ship) and it marked the end of uninterrupted Gaeldom in Ireland.

Amongst those who left with O'Neill was a young Ulsterman named Tagdh O'Cianain (Timothy Keenan) and he was to travel with the Earl through France and on to Rome. There O'Neill hoped to raise support from the Pope for another rebellion in Ireland — an ambition which remained unfulfilled. During their travels, O'Cianain kept a detailed diary which reflected both his own mood and that of his companions. On reaching Senigallia on the Adriatic Coast — a fortified city owned by the Duke of Urbino — O'Cianain wrote:

> There is an excellent and pretty hostel outside the city. There is a very fine river and a daisy-covered, clover-flowered level wide green, very near to that hostel.

Reading between the lines it is not hard to see that O'Cianain and the others were experiencing one of the torments of political exile — homesickness. The country through which they travelled bore little resemblance to the green fields of Ulster which O'Cianain knew. For that reason, the shamrock-covered bank is worthy of note in his diary. The clover and the shamrock were already becoming the symbols of longing and exile, reviving memories of Ireland for those gone from its shores.

Back in seventeenth-century Ireland, however, times had changed. The lands abandoned by the Gaelic lords had been confiscated and given over to English settlers. The country was, once again, slipping into an uneasy peace.

There is no doubt that the incoming English found their Irish neighbours rather strange and their ways even stranger. Much of the land had been doled out to Protestant settlers whilst many of the Irish tenantry remained staunchly Catholic. To many of the settlers Ireland was a foreign country with a foreign people, foreign religion and foreign habits. Few of those who took land had actually been to Ireland before and much of their 'knowledge' about the place had been gained through reading books or pamphlets — mainly English propaganda which had been circulated during the O'Neill rebellion. None of these sources had shown the Irish in a particularly complimentary light. Some of the English undoubtedly tended to regard the Irish as their social inferiors and little above animals.

For evidence of this latter opinion they claimed that they had to look no further than Irish dietary habits. The majority of English settler food tended to be cooked — and well cooked

at that — and was primarily meat-based, whereas the Irish seemed to have a taste — inexplicable to the English mind — for raw vegetables and herbs which they could pull from the hedgerows and fields. Whatever about the healthiness of the Irish diet, to English eyes, the Irish were only a little way above goats and cattle.

What was altogether shocking to the English was the idea that the Irish appeared to consume clover and shamrocks with some gusto! This may well have been the case, for the plants were readily available in the hedgerows and bushes and might have been used as a condiment to flavour stale or unappetising foods, in much the same way that parsley is used today. They might also have been used, as has been suggested, to 'sweeten the breath' and, in the days before any reliable dentistry, to disguise the unpleasant odour of rotting teeth. There is also some tentative evidence that the Irish may have eaten shamrocks soaked in whiskey as a treat at local festivals and gatherings.

Although herbs and plants were used in English cooking, they were usually added to give flavouring or spice to cooked meat, fowl or fish. Wild herbs were used as the basis for sauces and garnishes to enhance the taste of meats. Only animals and the utterly destitute ate the plants in their raw state from the fields and roadsides. Therefore, to see the Irish doing it served to confirm the centuries of prejudice concerning the perceived barbarity of Irishmen which had existed in England since the days of Geraldus Cambrensis in the twelfth century.

Alongside this cultural difference, and probably because of it, there was much studied debate as to what sort of plant the shamrock actually was. If the Irish ate it (and if the Irish were not terribly far removed from animals), it stood to reason that it was some form of 'grass', whereas if the Irish were to be allowed at least some degree of humanity, it might be considered as a 'cress' (which English cooks used). Undoubtedly, the debate as to the classification of the plant was heavily influenced by English cultural and political perceptions of the time. It might, it was generally thought, be more prudent to show the Irish as being no more than grass-eating cattle. If they were bestial by nature,

The Figure Hibernia on the O'Connell Monument, Dublin. On her head is a wreath of shamrocks.

it was up to the 'cultured' English to show them a better way (and to take their lands whilst doing so). Who could object to such a policy of 'education' and 'help'? And who at home in England could object to the killing of a few subhuman 'animals' if they were to rise in rebellion?

By now, the shamrock had begun to appear in the horticultural manuals and dictionaries under the Irish name seamróg. The first manuals were, in fact, Irish. One of the earliest mentions of the plant occurs in a manual written by Philib Ó Súilleabháin Beara, a native of County Cork who had been driven into exile in Spain during the early part of the seventeenth century. In 1620, he compiled a volume entitled *Zoilomastix*. This included chapters on plants with copious references to gardens in Connaught. One section dealt with what Ó Súilleabháin Beara described as *Trifolium*, in which he gave Greek, Latin, Spanish and Irish names for a 'three-leaved plant', whose Irish name is given as seamróg or seamur. However, there was no indication given as to its classification. Continental lexicographers and naturalists followed Ó Súilleabháin Beara's lead, referring to the plant simply as *Trifolium*. Rísteard Pluincéad's *Latin-Irish Dictionary* of 1662 noted that the plant *Trifolium* was the equivalent of Seamar and went so far as to distinguish *Trifolium acetosum* as seamróg. In 1768, O'Brien's *Herbal* listed seamróg and stated that it was a form of clover — the first official classification of the plant. He was followed by Connellan in 1804 and Ó Raghallaigh in 1821. This was both an Irish and Continental classification as clover. The English were not so sure.

The most widely accepted English classification was that of Matthias de L'Obel, a native of Flanders, who was responsible for the naming of the flower Lobelia. He had travelled to England in 1569 where his classifications of plants drew interest in the highest circles. Eventually, he obtained from James I, King of England, the title Botanicus Regius (King's Botanist). Around 1570, he collaborated with another Frenchman, Pierre Pena, a native of Aix-en-Provence, on a book called *Stirpium Adversaria Nova*. This was written in Montpellier and was dedicated to Queen Elizabeth I of England. Both de L'Obel and Pena classify the shamrock as 'grass'. They mention 'a certain gentleman of our acquaintance' who states:

> *The Meadow Trefoil . . . there is nothing better known or more frequent or more useful for the fattening whether of kine or beasts of burden. Nor is it from any other than the mere Irish, scorning all the delights and spurs of the palate, grind their cakes and loaves which they knead with butter and thrust into their groaning bellies.*

Following on this line, the English herbalist John Gerard refers in his *Herball of Generall Historie of Plants* (1597) to the 'Three Leafed Grasse or Meadow Trefoil'. This is classified as 'a grass'. The connection of the Meadow Trefoil with pigs or beasts of burden set an indelible image of the Irish within the English consciousness. This image was later developed by those who would define certain English policies in Ireland.

Whilst the argument as to the exact classification of the shamrock continued, events were rapidly overtaking it and were turning the plant into a more specific emblem of Irishness. The shamrock was becoming a cultural icon representing Irishness and, furthermore, was becoming more and more politicised in both the English and Irish minds.

Chapter Four

The Political Tradition

The first mention of the shamrock in an English text occurs in 1571 in a handwritten manuscript penned by the Elizabethan orator, scholar and Jesuit, Edmund Campion. Campion, who had written a number of extremely controversial pamphlets and articles which appeared to support Catholicism in Anglican England, was eventually hanged at Tyburn, London in 1581. He had journeyed to Ireland in August 1570 and had lived for several months as a virtual recluse in a house owned by Sir James Stanihurst, the Recorder of Dublin and Speaker of the Irish House of Commons. Although nominally an Anglican, Campion was strongly suspected of having 'Papist leanings' (and correctly so, since he was later to flee to Douai and become a Jesuit). He was therefore hounded by the English authorities and his visit to largely Catholic Ireland had to be conducted with a certain amount of secrecy. Even in Ireland, he was forced to move from house to house. During this time, he wrote the draft of his *Boke of the Histories of Ireland*, which was supposed to show how education was the only means by which the 'ignorant Irish' might be 'tamed'. At this time, Ireland was undergoing a series of rebellions against the English Crown, and Campion had decided to turn his not inconsiderable talents towards finding a solution to the Elizabethan 'Irish problem'. He completed his manuscript (intended to be his masterwork) on 9 June 1571 at a house in Drogheda.

Despite living in Ireland and having a number of Irish friends (admittedly from the Anglo-Irish nobility), Campion seems to have had little love for the common Irish, regarding them as 'wild' and badly in need of 'civilising'. He also viewed them as sly and cunning (which seems to have been a common English belief), ready to rise up in rebellion against their English betters like disobedient animals. He wrote:

> *Prowd they are of long and crisped glebes and the same doe nourishe with all their cunning. To crop whereof they take yt for a noble peece of vilany, shamrotes, watercresses, rootes and other herbes. They feed upon oatmeal and butter which they cram together. They drinke whea, milke and beiffe broth.*

'Shamrote' is simply one of the variants in English spelling used and can refer to no other growth but the shamrock.

Although he had intended his exposition on the Irish to be a printed masterwork, Campion did not publish it. He did, however, allow one of his pupils, Richard Stanihurst (the son of Sir James Stanihurst) to have unrestricted access to it. A wealthy Dubliner, Richard Stanihurst had studied at Oxford between 1563 and 1568, during the time that Campion was lecturing there, and the two had become friends. Nevertheless, Campion was rather unwise to let his former pupil study his unpublished work, for the latter copied large portions of it — some of which he took down unaltered and some of which he greatly embellished and changed — and later published them under his own name. One of the earliest statements that shamrocks were being eaten by the Irish as part of their diet appears under Stanihurst's name in Raphael Hollinshead's *Chronicles*, published in 1577, and undoubtedly owes much to Campion's original text.

A large section of Campion's *Boke*, now described as 'The Disposition and Maners of the Meere Irish (commonly called "the wylde Irish")' appeared as the eighth chapter of a work entitled *A treatise Contayning a Playne and Perfect Description of Irelande* by Richard Stanihurst, which was widely distributed in England. Stanihurst amended the original text to state that the Irish ate 'water cresses which they term as shamrocks'. In writing this, Stanihurst had, at a stroke, changed all commonly held botanical classifications of the plant and added to the confusion surrounding the shamrock. No longer was it either a 'grass' or a 'clover', but a 'cress'. This confusion would continue to reign for many years afterwards.

Although from Dublin himself, Stanihurst considered himself to be thoroughly 'Anglicised' and wrote quite disparagingly about the rural Irish who, he said, 'crammed their faces with shamrocks and roots'. This theme was quickly

taken up and expanded upon by other English writers who saw the Irish as a rich source of popular mockery.

Speaking of Irish ways, the English poet Edmund Spenser wrote wonderingly:

> *If they [the Irish] found a plot of watercresses and shamrocks, there they flocked as to a feast.*

The poet and playwright John Derricke also wrote in his 'Image of Ireland with a Discoverie of Wood Kearne' (a lengthy poem which contains the Epistle Dedicatorie and, although dated 16 June 1578, was not published until 1581):

> *For (in verie troth), my harte abhorreth their dealyngs and my soule doeth deteste their wilde shamrock manners.*

Derricke had, poetically, switched the word shamrock from being the name of a plant to a term of denigration referring specifically to the Irish. This descriptive term would also be used, in exactly the same way, during the period of the Irish Rebellion and the Irish Confederate Wars of the mid-1600s. The connection between the Irish diet, temperament and country was becoming increasingly firm.

In 1596, an anonymous play, staged in London, seemed to strengthen the connections between what the Irish ate and their rebellious and wayward nature. It suggested that the shamrock was 'rebel food', sustaining the armies who waged continual war against the English and their objectives in

Ireland. *The Famous Historye of the Life and Death of Captaine Thomas Stukely* was a satire on Ireland itself, on rebellion and on Irish politics and military prowess. Stukely was a celebrated English privateer who had persuaded the Pope to finance a small fleet to fight for the Catholic Fitzgeralds during the Geraldine Rebellion in Munster and had then proceeded to use it to invade Morocco on behalf of the King of Portugal. The play was filled with reflections on rebellion and upon the stupidity of the Irish. It contains the following extract which is supposedly set during a rebel attack on an English garrison at Dundalk. The O'Hanlon mentioned in the text is cited as one of the rebel leaders:

> O'HANLON: *Omarafasrot [bad cess], shamrocks are no meat.*
> *Nor bonny clabbo, nor greene water-cresses. Nor*
> *our strong butter, nor our strong oatmeale and*
> *drinking water brings them to the flixe.*

The term 'bonny clabbo' is taken to mean another so-called 'rebel food' — *bainne clabair* (literally 'milk mud' — buttermilk mixed with a little oatmeal).

The play was performed in taverns and playhouses and was widely seen and greatly appreciated by the inhabitants of London. Among those who came to see it were several English Members of Parliament, and it was mentioned in several speeches to the House as a justification for keeping armed troops garrisoned in Ireland at public expense. The argument was that 'the wild Irish', their passions inflamed by a diet of oatmeal and shamrocks, would attack all English settlers in the country and might even cross the Irish Sea and attack England itself!

Seeing the success of the 'Stukely' play, other writers were quick to jump on the anti-Irish bandwagon and some of them had no wish to hide behind the cloak of anonymity. Edward Sharpham's *The Fliere*, which was performed at Blackfriars by the Children of the Revels around 1605 or 1606, scathingly mocks 'two visitors from the Irish nation' — Master Oscabetha, the Irishman (*Uisce Beatha* — whiskey) and Shamrough, his lackey. So clownishly popular were these characters that they appeared in several other productions in taverns around London. Both were witless buffoons — the drunken Oscabetha shamelessly beat the unfortunate Shamrough around the stage whilst the latter whined and complained, much to the delight of the audiences. The Irish name of the plant was steadily being Anglicised into a word which combined 'sham' (false) and 'rogue' (villain).

However, things were not going at all well for the English in Ireland, either politically or militarily. In 1641, another rebellion broke out, starting in the north but quickly spreading to the south. Fearing that the Plantation of Ulster would lead to a general massacre of the Catholics there, many Catholics rose to protect themselves and to reclaim the lands of the Gaelic nobility, which had been confiscated by the

English after the Flight of the Earls. The rebellion was led by Sir Phelim O'Neill, a poor and indecisive commander who soon lost total control of the uprising. Individual militia captains both north and south, both Catholic and Protestant, were more or less left to their own devices, and the result was a bloodbath in which both sides — Catholic rebels and Protestant settlers — were horribly massacred. More troops were moved into Ireland from across the Irish Sea.

News, suggestions, rumours and downright lies filtered back across to England, each speaking of greater atrocities being daily committed upon the English by the 'wilde and unprincipled Irish'. England was quickly turning towards fundamentalist Protestantism and the undoubtedly exaggerated tales concerning its 'Popish' neighbour were readily believed. Suddenly Master Oscabetha the Irishman and his whining servant Shamrough didn't seem so funny to the English any more.

This was the age of the printed pamphlet, and anyone who wished to circulate their views, no matter how bizarre, could do so (provided that they could meet the cost). Pamphlets were, in fact, an early form of newspaper, sold mainly in London, but reaching other parts of England as well, and they certainly were a useful means of circulating the news from Ireland as it came in. However, lies, half-truths, personal opinions and gossip were also circulated. To offset the relatively high cost of printing by achieving a wider circulation, some pamphleteers took delight in the imagined gory details of what was allegedly happening in Ireland. And since a good number of pamphlets tended to be published anonymously, no one could really be held to account for the spurious 'news' that they conveyed.

One such pamphlet entitled *Grave News from Ireland* (1641) told how the Irish ate their own children in the style of savages and how they gorged themselves on the fattened off-spring of English settlers, roasting them on spits over open fires and then garnishing their blackened carcasses with herbs and shamrocks. Another publication — *Smoke from the Bottomless Pit or the Papists' True Purpose Discerned* (1642) — described in lurid detail imagined massacres in the north where hundreds of innocent English were bloodily massacred by Irish militiamen who wore Saint Patrick's Crosses and sprigs of shamrock attached to the bridles of their horses. Undoubtedly there were outrages committed by both sides in Ireland but these were greatly exaggerated by the pamphleteers whose accounts were accepted without question.

England itself was in political turmoil. Numerous con-frontations between a Puritan Protestant parliament and a king who was widely believed to have Catholic sympathies were edging the country closer to civil war. It was widely assumed that if such a war should break out, the King would raise an army in Ireland to attack the English Parliamentary forces. Several prominent Irish nobles, including the Earl of Antrim, had already declared for the King.

In a letter to the King dated 20 March 1638, the Earl stated that he would lead an army in support of the Royalist cause, which would 'feed their horses with the leaves of trees and themselves with shamrocks'. How a Royalist army could subsist on shamrocks is beyond imagination but the subsequent 'discovery' of the letter served to confirm the plant as 'rebel food'.

During and following the Cromwellian period in Ireland, the pamphlets circulating in London adopted an even more ferocious attack on the 'canniballe Irish'. Rough woodcuts, used to illustrate the spurious text, showed almost bestial creatures tearing unborn infants from their mothers' wombs and devouring them — 'laced with Oscabeatha and shamrogues'.

They will take the smallest children of Protestants and, cramming theire mouthes with shamrotes, hay and other grasses for to tenderise their meate, place them upon a soldier's pike which they hold over an open fire and when the poor unfortunate is so roasted they commence to devour the flesh of the children which they find exceptionally sweete and toothsome.

'New Horrors from Irelande, being a true account of the excesses of the canniballe Irish perpretrated and committed against the English in that country. Faithfully recounted by a gentleman.'

Such lurid accounts were undoubtedly used to justify the ferocity of the Cromwellian Army in Ireland as they ruthlessly crushed all opposition to English rule. They planted in the English mind a picture of bestial Irishmen wolfing down human flesh, tenderised with shamrocks and clover. This myth remained current even after the Restoration in 1660.

These dubious accounts aside, there is no doubt that English scholars now considered the shamrock as an integral part of the Irish diet. Dr Henry Mundy's pamphlet on dietary matters, written in 1680, notes:

> *The Irish . . . nourish themselves with their shamrock (which is a purple clover) and thus are swift of foot and of nimble strength.*

Similarly, writing from Tristernaght Abbey in County Westmeath around 1682, Sir Henry Piers, an English noble-man from Thomond, County Clare, says:

> *. . . butter, new cheese and curds and shamrocks are the food of the meaner sort'*

The confusion prevailing in England encouraged a surge of nationalistic fervour elsewhere. In Scotland, there was a distinct revival of patriotism, which translated itself into military action in an attempt to break away from England and Anglicanism. In Wales too, there was a sudden burst of anti-English activity. Welsh insurrectionists took to wearing daffodils upon the lapels of their jackets as a symbol of national pride. There was an old and persistent legend that Dewi Sant — Saint David, the Patron Saint of Wales — had been born in the Kingdom of Daffyd from which the daffodil came. (The wearing of the leek is probably of much older and more pagan origin.) In an imitation of their Welsh counterparts, the Irish began to forsake the Christian Saint Patrick's Cross and took to wearing shamrocks as a token of their defiance against the English.

In his book *A Treasury of Irish Folklore*, Padraic Colum states the following:

> *. . . Irish people wore the shamrock because it had a resemblance to a cross, its association with the Trinity is through an afterthought.*

Once again, English pamphleteers began to speak about the 'vile shamrock ways' of the Irish. And this time, they spoke with some justification, for the remnants of the old Catholic and Protestant militiamen still roamed through the countryside burning English estate houses and robbing the wealthy of their possessions. They styled themselves 'rapparees' or 'tories' (from an ancient Irish term for 'outlaw'). Several of these bands seem to have adopted the shamrock as their symbol. It was said, for example, that one of the most celebrated seventeenth-century highwayman in Ireland — 'Count' Redmond O'Hanlon who operated in the counties of Down, Armagh and Tyrone — wore a cockade of shamrocks in the band of his hat, as did several members of his gang, whilst Colonel Dudley Costello (whose gang burned English manor-houses in the Tyrone/Monaghan area) also wore a shamrock pinned to his lapel. In both English and Irish eyes, the shamrock was now seen as the mark of rebellion, of separation from England and of outlawry.

In 1689 an anonymous poem, printed in London by Randal Taylor (Publisher), was circulated throughout the city. It was entitled 'The Irish Rendezvous or a description of T.. ....ll's army of Tories and Bog-trotters', and was a scathing satire against the Earl of Tyrconnell who was supposed to be plotting another rebellion against English domination in Ireland. It contains the following lines:

> *Of Irish Tories and Scallogues,*
> *Arch as e'er trotted bog in Brogues,*
> *And of their mantles and their Trouses,*
> *Wherein full many a hungry louse is,*
> *I mean to sing 'Help me, St. Patrick,*
> *Or else I'll serve thee a trick,*
> *For I wear thy Cross and Shamrogue,*
> *Next seventeenth of March, I am a Rogue'.*

This was actually the first recorded reference to the wearing of shamrock on Saint Patrick's Day. Formerly 'rebel food' and used for sustaining insurrectionist armies, shamrocks were now becoming associated with the gluttony and debauchery of Saint Patrick's Day. As early as 1556 or 1557, the Lord Deputy of Ireland, Sir Henry Sidney, had stated that the Irish:

. . . surfeited upon their patron day, which is celebrated for the most part of the people of this country both with gluttony and idolatry as far as they dare.

There is little doubt that Saint Patrick's Day — 17 March — was a time of great feasting and drunkenness, particularly amongst the rural Irish. The date had been formalised by a Welshman — Edward Jones — who in 1794 had written a version of the legend of Saint Patrick which firmly fixed 17 March as the date of his death. Prior to this, the Feast of Saint Patrick had been part of the Easter festivities (Easter being taken as the date when the saint had converted the pagan Laoghaire, High King of Ireland, on the Hill at Tara, using the shamrock to explain the Godhead), although in Dublin it had been kept as 17 March for many years.

Following the success with London audiences of the *Irish Rendezvous*, other works appeared, which continued to show the Irish as perpetually drunken and extremely stupid. The English playwright James Farewell lost no time in further ridiculing them. Hard on the heels of the *Irish Rendezvous*, he published his own work — *An Irish Hudibras or Fengallian Prince* (also published in 1689), described by one pro-Irish commentator as

Statue of Saint Patrick holding single shamrock.

'a work of foul imagination'. In this poetic work, he describes the ghosts of Irish heroes as:

> *Stalking about the Bogs and Moors,*
> *Together with their Dogs and Whores,*
> *Without a Rag, Trouses or Brogues,*
> *Picking of Sorrel and Sham-rogues.*

Farewell's work was a skit on Virgil's epic poem *Aeneid*. In it, his hero prepares to enter the Underworld and seeks advice from a nun who tells him:

> *There grows a Bunch of Three-leaved grass,*
> *Called by the Boglanders, Shamrogues,*
> *A present for the Queen of Shogues,*
> *Which thou must first be after fetching,*
> *But all the cunning's in the catching.*

There was much debate as to the true identity of the 'Queen of Shogues'. Some folklorists have claimed her to be a minor demon and have asserted that shamrocks might have been used in Ireland for the purposes of witchcraft, but it is probably no more than a common English word for something without substance in the real world. Farewell's play was widely acclaimed and attracted large audiences. The shamrock was used once again as an instrument for poking fun at the Irish.

By this time, the world was entering what has been called the Age of Enlightenment — a period of scientific and rational enquiry. Nothing was left without investigation and that included the shamrock. After so long as the butt of English jokes against the Irish, it was now placed under scientific gaze to determine exactly what sort of plant it was.

By the mid-1690s, John Gerard's 1597 classification of the plant as a 'three-leafed grasse or Meadow Trefoil' was being called into question. In a letter to a fellow botanist Tancred Robinson, dated 15 December 1699, the naturalist Edward Lhuyd defined the plant thus: 'Their Shamrug is but a common clover'. Yet, he was to contradict himself several years later when he classified Shamrog as 'a wood sorrel'. A certain amount of confusion concerning the growth was setting in once more.

Soon other naturalists and botanists had entered the debate. The foremost of them was the Reverend Caleb Threkeld, a Dissenting Protestant clergyman who lived in Francis Street in the heart of Old Dublin near Saint Patrick's Cathedral. Threkeld was a native of Cumberland who had come to Dublin from the Lake District in 1713 to practise as a physician and to preach. It should be noted that, although he lived in Dublin, Threkeld had no great love for the Irish, whom he considered to be drunken, uncultured and highly rebellious, like disobedient children. His sermons frequently made remarks about 'potatoes and patriotism'.

His contribution to the debate on the shamrock came in the form of a small pocket-sized book published in Dublin on Thursday, 26 October 1726, on the subject of the wild plants of Ireland, with 'improving comments' on the nature of the Irish people themselves. He called the book *Synopsis Stirpium Hibernicarum* and, after many pages haranguing the Irish for their dissolute ways and urging them to turn to God (and become Protestants), he finally turned his attention to Irish plants. This is his account of 'Irish clover':

Trifolium Pratense Album — White Flowered Meadow Trefoyl:

The Meadow Trefoyls are called in Irish shamrocks as Gerard writes in his Herball . . . The word Seamar Leaune and Seamar Oge being a signification in the same, the first signifying the Child's Trefoyle and the other being the Young Trefoyl to distinguish them from the Seamar Capuil or Horse Trefoyl as I suppose.

He goes on:

The plant is worn by the people in their hats upon the 17th Day of March yearly (which is now called St. Patrick's Day). It being the current tradition that by this Three-Leafed Grass, he emblematically set forth to them the Mystery of the Holy Trinity.

However that be, when they wet the Seamar-oge, they often commit Excess in Liquor which is not a right keeping of the Day to the Lord, Error generally leading to Debauchery.

From his Dublin pulpit, Threkeld drew great attention to the little volume and to 'the truths contained therein', which mainly consisted of fiery lectures to his congregation about the evils of 'drowning the shamrock' on Saint Patrick's Day. None of these lectures seemed to have any effect upon his listeners for the day was still as drunken and debauched as ever — in fact, increasingly so. Indeed, little seemed to have changed since John Taylor, known as 'the Water Poet' had penned the following verse in 1630 having witnessed the excesses of the Irish on Saint Patrick's Day:

Whilst all the Hibernian Kernes in multitudes,
Did feast with Shamrogues steeved in Usquebaugh.

Besides devouring whiskey-soaked shamrocks, the Irish appeared to be wearing them more and more in their coats as a symbol of defiance against English domination. However, Saint Patrick's Crosses — a Christian rather than a political symbol — were still common. The celebrated Jonathan Swift, Dean of Saint Patrick's Cathedral in Dublin, wrote to his beloved Stella in 1713:

The Irish folks were disappointed that the Parliament did not
meet today because it was St. Patrick's Day and the Mall was
so full of crosses that I thought that all the world was Irish.

There were moves afoot to incorporate Saint Patrick's Cross, with its red saltire, into the Union Flag. This was no doubt to prepare the ground in Ireland for the dissolution of the Irish Parliament under an Act of Union (which eventually came about in 1801). The final straw came when, around the mid-to late-1700s, English soldiers quartered in Dublin began to wear both the Saint Patrick's Cross and red ribbons on the Day, 'in honour of the saint'. Similarly, Irish troops garrisoned in England were allowed to wear their saint's cross, a custom which was taken up by a number of their English comrades. The very thought of Englishmen wearing the cross of an Irish patron saint, and of the emblem being incorporated into an English flag, was too much for many Irishmen who spurned the wearing of the cross altogether in favour of the shamrock. Soon, all Irishmen were wearing the plant as a sign of their separateness from England.

However, even the shamrock was not to escape some form of Anglicisation. In 1783, King George III created a new Order of Chivalry — 'The Most Illustrious Order of Saint Patrick'. It was officially established 'for the dignity and honour of Our Realm of Ireland' and was open to most members of the Irish nobility. In fact, it was a blatant scheme for enhancing Royal influence in Ireland and for bribing the Irish nobles to allow English policies through the Irish Parliament. The Order was instituted on 11 March 1783, and the first knights were installed on 17 March at a lavish ceremony in Dublin Castle.

There was little that was blatantly Irish about the appearance of these knights. Their cloak and robe were sky blue in colour (and not green, which was rapidly becoming the hue associated with Ireland), as was the ribbon which they wore about their necks. However, at their installation, each knight was presented with a badge to distinguish his Order. The badge bore the red cross of Saint Patrick, placed against a white background, which was also charged with a green trefoil bearing a crown on each leaflet and the motto 'Quis Separabit' together with the date MDCCLXXXIII. The trefoil was a shamrock and the Knights of Saint Patrick were the first to employ it as a badge.

There is no doubt that this Order was a sop to the Catholics since it was mostly the rather sparse Catholic nobility who joined its ranks. After the Act of Union, any English interest in the Order dwindled and it gradually became extinct. Its motto, however, was assumed in Northern Ireland by the Loyalist Paramilitary Force, the Ulster Defence Association (UDA) — proof that mottoes at least can successfully cross the religious divide there.

For a while, the shamrock, which had started out as symbol of Irish separateness and distinction, became in Dublin at least an emblem of English status and title employed by the 'Catholic Unionists' who bowed the knee to the English king. In the rural areas beyond the city, however, the shamrock was assuming an altogether different symbolism.

In the Irish countryside, an enclosure movement conducted by English landlords was underway. Common land, on which the Irish people had grazed their cows for centuries, was suddenly closed off to make way for sheep and cereal crops. The landowners, sensing that money was to be made by supplying both grain and wool to the fledgling Industrial Revolution in England, sought to conserve as much land as they could by closing off their land and driving their tenants away through high rents. Many of the landlords were themselves English and most of them were absentee owners, leaving their estates in the hands of unscrupulous agents who 'racked up' the rents as they saw fit. In those days, the tenants had no recourse to law and had to put up with their situation as best they could.

In response to the harshness of the times, some of them formed themselves into secret oath-bound societies, initially as a response to the enclosure movement, but gradually taking on a number of other social problems as well. These were vigilante groups whose sole action was to pull down enclosing fences, rob the landlord and his agents, and create mayhem for the greater majority of English-owned estates. Most of these groups were little more than outlaws who traced their political ancestry back to the localised militia bands of the mid-to late-1600s.

Not all of these bands were Catholic; a good many of them were composed of Presbyterians, who had as little love for the English and the established Anglican Church as had the

Catholics. One of the main secret societies of the time was 'The Peep O'Day Boys', so called because they transacted most of their business and settled most of their 'debts' at 'peep o' day' (daybreak). They were not a large and unified organisation, but rather a number of smaller groups, scattered throughout Ireland, some of whom maintained sporadic contact with each other. Several of these groups adopted the shamrock as their emblem, and as the 'Peep O'Day Boys' fractured and split they formed other groups such as 'The Shamrock Boys' in Wexford and Cork. Gradually, Catholics began to form their own groupings as well, many incorporating the word 'shamrock' into their titles.

Along the Monaghan/Cavan borders, the 'Hearts of Oak' and 'Hearts of Steel' flourished, some of them espousing the shamrock as their symbol, whilst in Tipperary and Galway, 'The Shamrock Defenders' harassed local landlords unmercifully. The English seemed to be powerless against them.

Among the most prominent of these groups were the 'Whiteboys' (so called because they wore white coats over their normal clothes when they went out on their nightly raids). This group operated in the countryside just outside Dublin and further north as well. Like the 'Peep O'Day Boys' they were a secretive vigilante band, operating in small, separate units, attacking isolated manor houses and robbing stagecoaches. Some of these groupings styled themselves 'The Shamrock Volunteers', as a mark of their separateness from, and their defence of, the Irish people against English rule. This group seems to have been particularly strong in the Armagh and Tyrone areas where they were almost exclusively Catholic. There were also some similarly named bands operating in the countryside just outside Dublin itself.

If the mid-1600s had been a politically turbulent time, the end of the 1700s was even more so. Events overseas such as the French Revolution and the American War of Independence were exciting the Irish population, both Catholic and Protestant. The English Government was, at this time, not at all popular in Ireland. Trade restrictions had been imposed and the Penal Laws had affected Presbyterians as well as Catholics, so there was little goodwill towards English authority from either faith. There was also a continual fear amongst Anglican merchants in Belfast and Dublin that rebels in the countryside would assist a French or American invasion of England. The whole climate of Ireland fairly seethed with anti-English feeling and was becoming politically highly charged.

Anglican mercantile fears intensified when the American frigate *Ranger*, under the command of Captain John-Paul Jones, appeared in Belfast Lough and captured a British sloop which was sent against it. When the northern port of Carrickfergus was held for five days by French pirates, led by a ruffian called Thurot, those living in the major trading towns realised that something had to be done. In response to these outrages, in 1779 Protestant merchants began to form armed militias, which they called Volunteers. Although the initial companies were formed in the Belfast area, the idea quickly spread throughout Ulster and Leinster and along many coastal regions of Ireland where local shipping was being harassed by American privateers based in French ports.

The Volunteers were in the main Protestant and took their orders from Anglicised landowners and merchants but there was a subtle undercurrent of rebellion about them. A good number of them were Presbyterians who objected to both the established Anglican Church and the trade restrictions which were crippling the Irish. As a symbol of their distinctiveness, many Volunteer companies adopted the shamrock as their emblem and displayed it on their flags and regalia. Amongst those who used it as part of their company colours were the Royal Glin Hussars (formed by the Knight of Glin, County Limerick, in July 1779), the Tullamore True Blues, the Limerick Volunteers and the Maguiresbridge Volunteers.

A sprig of shamrocks also appeared on the flag of the Castle Ray Fencibles, whilst the Loyal Volunteers of Cork paraded through the Mall of the city wearing sprigs of shamrock in their hats, as cockades. Eventually some of these would form the local militia factions ordered to suppress the rebellion of the United Irishmen in 1798, and there is some evidence that the shamrock crossed the 'political divide' and became a symbol of English oppression at this time. There is a persistent tradition that some of the Monaghan Militia, garrisoned at Blaris Moor near Lisburn, wore shamrock-cockades in their caps as they put down the insurgents at the Battle of Antrim on 7 June 1798. The plant also appears on the reverse side of a medal presented to the Armagh Protestant Volunteers for their part in putting down threatened local insurrections in the south of the county. The emblem was now becoming one of English mastery rather than Irish resistance.

There is little evidence that the shamrock was widely used as a symbol by the United Irishmen themselves. They did, however, carry green flags into several battles — 'the National flag of sacred green, an imitation of the shamrock' (Gordon). This was linked with the cry *'Erin go Brách'* (Ireland forever).

However, popular legend states that during the Battle of Antrim, several members of Jemmy Hope's 'Spartan Band' (a troop of insurgent musketeers who briefly held the Unitarian Meeting House in the town) sported bunches of shamrock tied to their weapons. Certainly, at the nearby Battle of Ballynahinch, the insurgents wore accoutrements which bore a harp entwined with a wreath of shamrocks, whilst a standard bearing a similar insignia was raised at the Creevy Rocks near the town on the orders of the Down insurgent leader, Henry Monroe.

Following the failure of the admittedly haphazard 1798 Rising, England took a little time to breathe easy. The spirit of rebellion, however, still flickered beneath the outward calm of Ireland. On 4 February 1799, with the Act of Union only a couple of years away, an anti-Union journal advocating outright and bloody rebellion appeared on the streets of Dublin to alarm the English authorities in the Castle. Its name was significantly *The Shamroc* and it bore a drawing of the plant as part of its masthead. The shamrock was now once again a symbol of rebellion and was increasingly becoming the representation of Ireland itself and of independence.

Whilst *The Shamroc* journal did very little to stir rebellion in Ireland where it had only a limited circulation, copies were widespread in Paris. Here, if tradition is to be believed, it found its way into the hands of a certain Robert Emmet, younger brother of the prominent United Irishman, Thomas Addis Emmet. Robert was a dreamer and an incurable romantic, and he had long harboured dreams of returning to Ireland and leading another full-scale rebellion.

Fancying himself something of a poet, Emmet would later pen a few lines in praise of the 'rebel plant':

The Shamrock was as lovely green,
In its early days as e'er was seen.

Emmet returned to Ireland and in 1803 led a shambolic rising, which failed almost as soon as it had begun. In his address to his followers at the Marshalsea Depot in Dublin, just prior to the rising, Emmet used the romantic imagery of the 'shamrock-crowned isle' to instil patriotic fervour. He soon lost control of the rebellion, which fizzled out after the cold-blooded slaying of Lord Kilwarden, and Emmet himself was captured and hanged.

The English remained uneasy about affairs in Ireland, even after the Act of Union was pushed through in 1801. Fresh satires about the Irish bogeyman across the water appeared in English playhouses and taverns once more. And once again, Master (now Captain) Oscabetha and his valet Shamrogue stepped onto the stage, mouthing treacherous epithets against English authority. The audience still laughed at them — in fact, Oscabetha remained a figure of fun until roughly about 1810 — but they now laughed at a much darker, more political humour than before. Oscabetha and Shamrogue remained the clowns — the foolish, drunken and incompetent commanders of an undisciplined rebel army — but they were now more threatening and sinister.

In the Irish countryside, there had been a revival of the oath-bound secret societies, closely allied with certain political factions such as the Young Ireland Movement, who agitated for land reform. Many of these took the shamrock as their emblem, and the plant was now also becoming associated with another political cause — that of Catholic emancipation. In fact, so closely was the shamrock now identified with emancipation that, during a Monster Rally at Mullaghmast in 1843,

Decoration from title page of The Spirit of the Nation *published in 1843.*

the 'Great Liberator', Daniel O'Connell, was presented with a drinking cup embroidered with shamrocks.

However, the symbolism of the shamrock was about to undergo another change as two great evils suddenly and unexpectedly gripped Ireland — the twin horrors of famine and emigration.

Chapter Five

The Artistic Tradition

In the autumn of 1845, the Irish potato crop failed. Potatoes had been the staple diet of the rural Irish for almost two centuries and the blight was devastating. Little was done to alleviate suffering within the country as the death toll mounted daily. Many found themselves forced to emigrate. Rural landlords, anxious to clear the land to make way for sheep, were happy to pay the £3 boat fare to America or Canada on unseaworthy ships. Those who took up the offer of emigration knew that they would never return.

They carried part of the country with them, as an image in their hearts. It is recorded that several also carried 'clods of earth' from their own townlands as keepsakes — the original 'oul' sod'. On some of these grew grasses and small flowers. Like Tagdh O'Cianain, two centuries before, many were probably already feeling the effects of homesickness, and wanted to have some emblem of their land close by them. And what plant would represent 'the oul' sod' more than the shamrock?

The Act of Union of 1801 had affected two different sets of people in rather different ways. Members of the old Protestant aristocracy, who had enjoyed power and prestige through the Irish Parliament, suddenly found themselves without status, as the Act abolished their former power base. They felt cut off from England and began to look towards a former golden Gaelic age to reassert themselves, claiming that they were, and had always been, Irish.

The Catholics too were outraged by the Act since the full Emancipation promised by Lord Castlereagh had never materialised. The King, George III, was implacably opposed to such a move, believing that it violated his Coronation Oath to uphold the established Church. Thus Emancipation seemed nothing more than a dream. Its supporters also began to look back towards a Golden Age of Gaeldom.

Many supporters of the Gaelic Revival were extremely literate Protestants. Foremost of these was William Smith O'Brien, a Unitarian, and something of an accomplished poet. He and his companions embarked on a 'consciousness raising' movement which became part of a Celtic Renaissance that swept not only Ireland but parts of England and Scotland as well. Suddenly it became fashionable to be conversant with Irish culture. Many of the Anglo-Irish gentry now professed themselves as experts in Irish poetry, writing, art and harp music. No longer was the Irishman viewed as an ignorant and drunken savage, but as the inheritor of ancient mystical traditions and lore. The shamrock, used as a decorative device, exemplified this new mood and thinking.

Apart from its appearance on badges and on political and military accoutrements, examples of the shamrock as decoration are relatively hard to find before 1800. The exceptions were, of course, some Volunteer standards, some United Irishmen flags and the badges of the Knights of Saint Patrick. From about 1810 onwards, however, trefoils (shamrocks) appear on almost every conceivable object from salt cellars to chamber pots.

A notable exception to the above was the decorative cornice mouldings in the hall of Glin Castle, County Limerick, ancestral home of the Knights of Glin. Here, shamrocks had been in evidence since the early 1780s and probably sprang from the Fitzgeralds' strong association with the Volunteer movement. In Limerick, the shamrock also appeared on a number of flags reputedly belonging to United Irishmen forces, but these are not thought to have influenced the mouldings in any way. Nor did any of the then current architectural designs seek to copy the decoration of Glin Castle, although at nearby Ash Hill Towers, shamrocks were incorporated into the stucco, probably by the same craftsman who worked at Glin. In Dublin, it is believed that the hallway of one of the town houses in Mountjoy Square was decorated with a frieze of shamrocks but this has probably been lost.

It was said too, that shamrocks once prominently decorated one of the stone urns topping the gate pillar leading into the now-disused Roman Catholic church in Oranmore, County Galway, but on closer inspection they have been shown to be no more than Scottish thistles and a crudely designed English rose. Why they should be there — and why they should be mistaken as shamrocks — is unknown.

Shamrocks really began to proliferate in Irish and Anglo-Irish art from around 1810 as the Celtic Renaissance gradually gripped the popular mind. With a developing interest in Irish music, many wealthier Dubliners turned their attention to Irish harp music. The most famous Dublin harp-maker was John Egan and, in keeping with the mood of the time, he began to turn out harps, lavishly decorated with (some might say 'splattered with') multitudes of shamrocks. Initially this may have been no more than a 'signature device', designed to distinguish Egan's work from that of other harp-makers (his initial harps simply had a shamrock marquetry on the sounding box, like a trademark), but it became very popular amongst the 'new Gaelic' classes who demanded representations of shamrocks all over their instruments.

In 1813, Thomas Moore's poem 'O The Shamrock' made its appearance, extolling the 'chosen leaf of bard and chief', and the shamrock's popularity seemed to be permanently assured.

Coins and tokens issued by Irish banks and companies — and some by the Royal Mint itself — began to incorporate the shamrock as part of their overall device. It was even mooted as early as 1804 by Sir Joseph Banks, the great naturalist and for many years the 'director' of Kew Gardens, that all Irish coinage should have on the reverse, a device composed of the Irish harp 'surmounted with a wreath of shamrock'. The Privy Council on Coinage rejected the idea in favour of Hibernia, because of the plant's 'rebellious connotations', but the agreed coinage was never actually produced. However, Banks' suggestion found some favour in 1813 when the Bank of Ireland issued a token overly festooned with shamrocks. The design was specified in the Parliamentary Act 53, (George III 106) which permitted minting:

> . . . *the said last-mentioned Tokens on the one Side of His Majesty's Head . . . and on the reverse Side thereof respectively, with a Wreath of Shamrock Leaves, the Words and Figures 'Bank Token 5 Pence Irish 1813'.*

The Bank of Ireland's lead was followed by a number of other private companies who adorned their own tokens with shamrocks — one example was the second-class railway token for the Dublin and Kingstown Railway. The last occasion on which the emblem was used on any coin issued in Ireland was in 1822 and 1823 when three shamrocks embellished the harp on the halfpenny and penny of King George IV. Both coins were withdrawn in 1826. By 1821, the coinage of both Ireland and England had been amalgamated and thereafter only Imperial coins issued by the Royal Mint in London were circulated in Ireland, the others being gradually withdrawn.

In 1821 Ireland also received an important visitor — King George IV of England. The King's visit was designed to stem the disquiet that had been simmering in Ireland following the failure to include the promised Catholic Emancipation in the Act of Union. The monarch spent a month in Ireland and was well received — particularly in Dublin — and professed himself very pleased with 'all things Gaelic'. The remark was meant to mollify the Catholic opposition to unification which bubbled just beneath the surface of Irish society but it had a much wider impact. Suddenly 'all things Gaelic' had Royal approval and the Celtic Renaissance took off. Tiny cushions, minutely stitched with shamrocks, appeared in 1817 with a fitting prayer also stitched into the fabric of a central panel to indicate the wishes of the maker:

To *Erin's land,*
With liberal hand,
Extend Your timely care,
The poor to feed,
n this their need,
From Your abundance spare.

It doesn't take much to see that such beautifully crafted items would fit well amongst the growing flow of emigrants who were reluctantly leaving the land of their birth.

An early example of book decoration which was also coming to the fore, is in a manuscript concerning the coats of arms of great Irish families. It was by Patrick Kennedy, Pursuivant of Athlone. Kennedy's title distinguished him as one of the Heraldic Officers of Dublin Castle, and so his book was an important one. He completed the work entitled *The Book of Arms* in 1816 but it was not published until 1967. His manuscript contains sketches of Irish arms and the hand-drawn border of the title page is composed of shamrocks.

In the world of heraldry, Kennedy was taking a bold step. Shamrocks do not appear at all in ancient Irish heraldry. Although there are certainly a number of heraldic devices which incorporate pointed leaflets, these cannot even be equated with trefoils or the shamrock plant. Where shamrocks were employed they were simply for decoration and not as an essential piece to the device itself. For example, decorations of shamrocks and palms appear on the bookplate of Leonard McNally, a rather devious barrister who represented several of the United Irishmen in the Dublin Courts and at the same time betrayed them by passing on relevant information about them to the authorities.

The artistic representation of the plant was also entering another field — that of architecture. It was the O'Shea brothers who started the fashion in Dublin of incorporating shamrocks into carvings around the doors and windows of the grand houses. They detailed a series of immature flower buds interspersed with trefoils on the architraves of windows and on one of the entrances to the building which was originally the Kildare Street Club, to accompany the rather risqué ornamentation of monkeys playing snooker. The shamrocked doorway now leads to the offices of the Chief Herald of Ireland.

Shamrocks were also appearing on documents granting armorial bearings to Trinity College, Dublin. It made perfect sense that the 'College of the Holy and Undivided Trinity' should have at least some representation of the three-leafed plant, representing both pagan Gaelic and Christian learning and tradition. However, the shamrocks which appear on the official document are not part of the University's armorial device, rather they are technically what is known as a 'conceit' — merely an added decoration.

Artistically linking the shamrock with Catholic Emancipation, the second Earl of Rosse (1758–1841) emblazoned the tower of Saint Brendan's Church in Birr, County Offaly, with shamrocks and trefoils, to draw attention to the issue of Emancipation of which he (the Earl) was a prominent architect. Other churches and their patrons rushed to follow

the Earl's example. The most lavish decoration appears in the Roman Catholic church at Kilcock in County Kildare, where ecclesiastical shamrocks appear, arranged in groups of four, together with harps, on the church reredos.

However, it was emigration, both from the ravages of unemployment in the north during the 1830s and from the Famine-stricken south in the 1840s, that really brought the shamrock to the fore. Emigration, which had started as a tiny trickle in the early 1700s, now became a raging torrent.

The majority of those who left would never see Ireland again, and they and their children would eventually provide a market for all things Irish — including the shamrock. Many prospective manufacturers were quick to seize upon this symbol of Ireland. And, in investigating the potential American market, another group with an interest in the shamrock came to light — the Scots.

Although not as firmly established in Scottish culture as in Irish, the plant figured peripherally in Caledonian lore. According to Scottish tradition, Saint Columcille (the Scottish Saint Columba) had brought the shamrock from Ireland to Scotland on the hem of his robe (echoing Saint Patrick who reputedly brought it to Ireland in the soles of his sandals). As in Ireland, it was predominantly associated with

Nationalistic fervour and particularly with the Jacobite cause. Nicholas Sweetman, the eccentric eighteenth-century Bishop of Ferns in Wexford, had preached rousing sermons linking 'the shamrock and the thistle' in support of the Jacobites, and there had also been strong connections in the north between the two plants through the offices of the MacDonnells of Islay who held land in North Antrim. One tradition stated that when the blind Irish harper, Denis O'Hempsey (described as the 'last true bard of Ireland') played for Charles Edward Stuart at Holyrood, the aged musician handed the Jacobite Prince a sprig of shamrock as a symbol of the sympathies of the people of Ireland for his cause. In reply, the Prince handed O'Hempsey the white cockade from his bonnet.

Thus, the shamrock appealed not only to the American-Irish but also to emigrant Scots in America who had come there fleeing clearances and famine in their own country.

Taking advantage of both Irish and Scottish markets overseas, merchants, artisans and exporters began shipping off mass-produced goods for sale in the developing American society. Shamrocks intertwined with thistles and roses were painted upon goblets, dishes, glassware and furniture, and boxes appeared in New York, Boston, Philadelphia and San Francisco. Tables, carved from local woods, were made largely in Killarney for export oversees. Fake bog oak was also used for inlay. These pieces, known as 'Killarney-ware', despite

their shamrockery (or shamroguery), still represent some of the best furniture ever produced in Ireland.

The Belleek Pottery in County Fermanagh also went into the shamrock-style export market. It sent tea services, pots, butter dishes and bowls, all of which were embellished with a mixture of hand-painted shamrocks, wild flowers, harps and wolfhounds. In America they were snapped up by eager collectors. There is still a great interest in the Belleek range today, especially those with shamrocks painted on them. In the nineteenth century, no Irish-American dinner party was complete without shamrock-entwined decanters, probably bearing the legend 'Erin go brágh', or 'To the immortal Memory of William III' (where a horse and rider were often surrounded by shamrock wreaths). In this, the shamrock moved freely across political and religious divides.

In the popular mind, the shamrock still had not lost its 'rebel' status and this, no doubt, contributed to its 'Irishness' amongst those Americans who disapproved of British policy back in Ireland. Shamrocks had been carved upon the grave marker of Father Nicholas Sheehy at Clogheen, County Tipperary. Sheehy was hanged for his involvement with the United Irishmen, and his grave was seen as a great icon of rebellion. Small representations of his gravestone wreathed with shamrocks were also

John Keegan Casey's memorial in Glasnevin Cemetery.
Courtesy Peter Costello

on sale amongst the American-Irish and were readily snapped up. Carved shamrocks, too, adorned the funeral monument of John Keegan Casey at Glasnevin Cemetery. Casey had been a notorious Fenian sympathiser and in 1866 had written a number of ballads and poems under the title 'A wreath of shamrocks'. Pictures of his tomb surrounded by shamrocks sold very well in America. Similarly, brooches designed in the style that Robert Emmet had reputedly given to his sweetheart Sarah Curran were on sale in many Irish jewellers. This adornment was formed in the shape of a harp with a wreath of shamrocks above it. This was very popular with Irish-American 'ladies of quality' — the damsels of the old Irish families who had 'made good' in the New World.

The Parnell Monument at the north end of O'Connell Street in Dublin is decorated about its base with shamrocks, whilst the figure of Hibernia on the O'Connell Monument at the opposite end of the street wears shamrocks on her brow.

It was not really these 'revolutionary symbols', however, which made the shamrock known worldwide. Rather it was the Anglo-Irish aristocracy of Victorian times who extolled the virtues of the plant and who brought it to the attention of designers. Victorian ladies as far apart as London and Boston wore gowns made in Limerick and Cork, the fabric of which was festooned with depictions of hand-embroidered shamrocks. These ladies, who now styled themselves 'Irish belles', could also wear necklaces, pendants, brooches and rings styled as shamrocks. Tapestries too — some designed from 'Irish diamonds' (iron pyrites) and set against black backgrounds — tastefully dominated Victorian drawing rooms. These depicted motifs as diverse as shamrocks, harps, ancient Irish heroes, dreaming bards and fairy folk, and were considered to be an 'essential' home decoration for any pseudo-Irish family worth its salt. Solid gold shamrock ornaments were available for as little as twenty-five shillings at the latter end of the nineteenth century.

Another export that was taking America and London by storm was Irish linen. Tablecloths, napkins, antimacassars and even handkerchiefs were all being made from linen, all embroidered or covered in Celtic motifs — most notably harps and shamrocks. And if an Irishman of noble birth wished to mop his brow with his shamrock-embroidered handkerchief, he could do so while seated in a rather questionable 'bog-oak' chair lavishly inscribed with harps and shamrocks. And when he went to close his curtains to keep away the light from his eyes, these too could be emblazoned with shamrocks and harps.

If the shamrock was lavishly depicted for most of the year, it really came into its own on Saint Patrick's Day. The 1880s were the age of the postcard and this was the one item guaranteed to fulfil the needs of the homesick Irish emigrant. Postcards were cheap and easy to post, and greetings, news and gossip could travel back and forth across the Atlantic with little difficulty. The heyday of the picture postcard was the early years of the twentieth century and what better picture of Ireland to send than a shamrock?

Initially, the cards were simply pieces of board with a shamrock — dried and pressed — glued to them. Others had shamrocks drawn on them. Soon these were on sale everywhere, ready for posting, and were gleefully sent off on Saint Patrick's Day from Boston, New York, Chicago and other places where the Irish had settled. Gradually, the cards became more sophisticated, more glossy and much more expensive. Lines of poetry — particularly the Thomas Moore ballad 'O the Shamrock' — were printed on cards, and were wreathed in shamrocks. These were sent as a form of greeting.

Detail from The Parnell Monument at Parnell Square.

It was a small step from printing cards to printing books, pamphlets and song sheets. There was nothing that the Irish abroad liked to do more than sing — usually tearful, misty-eyed songs of exile and longing. Pubs and Irish clubs in London, Glasgow and various American cities were filled with musicians and singers who wanted to give of their best — but they needed the music. To increase its appeal, the printed music had to be illustrated and embellished. The accompanying illustrations often reflected the sentimentality of the song itself and drew upon stereotyped images of a land most of the singers had never seen. Thus the popular song 'Mother Mo Chroí' bore an illustration of an old woman, wrapped in a Galway shawl, standing by the door of a thatched cottage where shamrocks sprouted. The music itself, together with the words, was wrapped with swathes of shamrocks. Song sheets of such 'patriotic' ballads as 'The Minstrel Boy' boasted a similar 'shamroguery' on their covers. Much later, popular song sheets of melodies such as 'My Wild Irish Rose' and 'I Dreamed Last Night I was in Erin' maintained this theme with cover illustrations of pretty colleens skipping through sunlit fields of shamrocks. Daniel Maclise's edition of Moore's *Irish Melodies* (published in 1845) boasted beautiful representations on several pages of shamrocks and harps.

Soon Irish history books were also adopting frontispieces bordered by wreaths of shamrocks, and dust jackets upon which the plant appeared in some profusion. One of the first of these was Lord Castlehaven's *Memoirs of the Irish Wars*, published in 1815 by the Dublin company of George Mullen and Sons. To appeal to the widest possible market, Mullen used a combination of oak leaves (a predominantly English symbol) and shamrocks to decorate the leather binding of the work.

By the end of the century, shamrocks were appearing on the bindings of any book of Irish interest as well as on endpapers, frontispieces and dust jackets. Official publications that concerned, or were destined for, Ireland, used the emblem of the shamrock. This was to vanish when the Irish Free State was established in 1922, but there was a small resurgence of the practice in Irish Government circles during the 1970s.

Shamrocks were even used as borders for printed texts within the books themselves. The most striking examples of this are the decorations of shamrocks and trefoils designed by Holden, which augment many of the pages of the illustrated edition of William Carleton's *Traits and Stories of the Irish People*. Here, the shamrock fits in well with the 'folkloric' themes running through the book and

The Four Provinces Postage Stamp.

blends tastefully with the text. Many other decorations were not so tasteful. The cover papers of a popular edition of Lady Morgan's *The Wild Irish Girl* was positively littered with shamrocks when it appeared in America in the 1930s.

Since then, the shamrock has become a firm feature of the Irish tourist market. It appears, etched upon the sides of everything from butter dishes and milk jugs to delicate porcelain. It is still to be found on Irish tea towels, cushions, tablecloths and place mats, and decorates the borders, spines and endpapers of certain Irish books.

Whilst shamrock-embroidered ball gowns have largely disappeared, it is still possible to buy shamrock-covered coats and waistcoats in New York coming up to Saint Patrick's Day. It is probably true to say that the shamrock is still as fixed in the Irish psyche today as it ever was in the past. And it seems just as marketable in the modern world as it was in the 1800s. It has become the perennial symbol of the Irish abroad.

Conclusion

It is probably true to say that no other plant is so intertwined with both the history and folklore of Ireland as the shamrock. That association has been both a varied and complicated one. From its (admittedly speculative) beginnings as a pagan symbol representing the Triple-Goddess of the ancient Celts, it has gone on to become the embodiment of Irish Christian history and tradition, inextricably linked with the Irish patron saint, Patrick. From being the focus of Irish mockery against the Irish, it eventually became the epitome of Anglo-Irish culture and sophistication. It has been used by saints, playwrights, churchmen and kings. From being significantly absent in ancient texts and artwork, it has blossomed into a symbol of Ireland in many products and representations of the country. It has been extolled in song, story and poem.

Today's commercial use of the shamrock both as a logo and as something of a tourist gimmick has tended to trivialise its symbolic value. It is hard to consider the plant in all its complexities when it forms the centre of an everyday table mat. It is difficult to take it as a potent symbol when its shape is being poured as the head of a pint of Guinness by a New York barman. And yet there is still something of that deep and

ancient symbolic power surrounding the shamrock. This is certainly very evident in the still staunchly Unionist Northern Ireland where many still consider it as a symbol of rebellion, of hostile Catholicism and of anti-English Gaeldom. Amongst many Unionists, the shamrock is still viewed as an object of scorn, just as it was in sixteenth- and seventeenth-century England. However, it is interesting to note that the badge of the Royal Ulster Constabulary includes a British Crown, surmounted upon two wreaths of shamrocks.

The Logo of Aer Lingus, the Irish National Airline.
Courtesy Aer Lingus

The growth still retains something of its superstitious power as well. A four-leafed shamrock (known as Mary's Shamrock and widely considered as something out of the ordinary when set against its three-leafed companions) is considered extremely lucky and whoever finds one will reputedly gain great financial rewards coupled with worldly success. Consequently, even in this cynical, modern-day world, many people still go on the hunt for four-leafed shamrocks in the hopes of winning the Lotto or gaining some favourable contract. This probably says more about the rarity of the plant (all rare objects are considered to be lucky) as the same is also said about four-leafed clover and some varieties of heather.

This is one of the very few books ever to have been written about the shamrock and it has tried to place the plant in its historical, artistic and literary contexts, but a great deal more work needs to be done before the whole picture of this enigmatic and vastly symbolic plant can emerge.

Perhaps the final word on the shamrock should be left to an intriguingly (although, one hopes, not descriptively) named singer — Miss Mountain — who sang the following verse, culled from Croften-Croker's *Popular Songs of Ireland*, each night at the Opera House in Capel Street, Dublin:

This plant that blooms forever,
With the Rose Combined,
And the Thistle twined,
Defies the strength of foes forever.

Bibliography

Anonymous, *The Famous Historye of the Life and Death of Captaine Thomas Stukely*, 1596.

Anonymous, *New Horrors from Irelande, being a true account of the excesses of the canniballe Irish perpetrated and committed against the English in that country. Faithfully recounted by a gentleman,* — Thomasyn Tracts, London: 1651.

Briggs, Katharine, *A Dictionary of Fairies*, 1976.

Campion, Edmund, *First Boke*, 1571.

Colgan, 'The Shamrock in Literature' in the *Journal of the Proceedings of the Royal Society of Antiquaries of Ireland*, 1897.

Colum, Padraic, *A Treasury of Irish Folklore*, 1962.

Derricke, *Image of Ireland*, 1581.

Dinely, Thomas, *Journal*, 1681.

Fitzgerald, The Reverend and T.P. McGregor, *History, Topography and Antiquities of Limerick*, Dublin: 1826–7.

Glassie, Henry. *Passing the Time in Ballymenone: Folklore and History of an Ulster Community*, Philadelphia/Dublin: 1982.

Gordon, *History of the Rebellion*, 1803.

Hood, A.B.E. (ed), *St. Patrick, his writings and Muirchu's Life*, 1978.

Journal of the Cork Historical and Archaeological Society: 1895.

O'Cianain, Tagdh,*The Flight of the Earls*, trans. Fr Paul Walsh, 1916.

Piers, Sir Henry, *A Chronological Description of the County of Westmeath*, 1774.

Sidney, quoted by Flood in 'The Month', 1921.

Spenser, *A View of the State of Ireland*, 1580.

Threkeld, *Synopisis Stirpium*, 1726.